The Man Who Built Churches

The Story of B.D. Stevens
A parable for our time

Edited and illustrated by Peter W. Brock

Pottersfield Press, Lawrencetown Beach,
Nova Scotia

Copyright 1990 Peter W. Brock

Canadian Cataloguing in Publication Data

Brock, Peter W.

   The man who built churches

      ISBN 0-919001-64-5

1. Stevens, B.D. 2. Baptists - Nova

Scotia - Biography. 3.Baptists - Nova

Scotia - History - 20th Century. 4.

Churches, Baptist - Nova Scotia - History -

20th century. I. Title

BX6495.S77B76 1990 286.'1'092   C90-097611-X

Published by
Pottersfield Press
R.R. 2, Porters Lake,
N.S. BOJ 2SO

Published with the assistance of the Canada Council and The
Nova Scotia Department of Tourism and Culture

This book is a work of oral history and, while every effort has been
made to convey an accurate rendering of events, the publisher
reminds the reader that the story herein is based on interviews
with a wide range of people, and opinions expressed do not
necessarily reflect the views of the publisher.

Printed on acid-free paper made of recycled fibre.

Contents

Cast of Characters
in order of appearance.

BD . . . . . Himself.

Laurie Stevens . . . . . BD's son.

Art Smith . . . . . lawyer.

Blair Williams . . . . . foreman in Fredericton.

Helen Thompson . . . . . BD's eldest daughter.

Wayne Langley . . . . . former labourer and now an IBM executive.

Andrew Levy . . . . . heating contractor.

Harry Renfree . . . . . pastor, Mulgrave Park Church, and official historian of the Baptist Church in Canada, now living in Victoria, B.C.

Reg Short and Betty Short . . . . . purchased their first home from BD.

Rhodes Cooper . . . . . pastor of the St. Philip's Anglican Church.

Abner Langley . . . . . pastor and past director of the Divinity College, Acadia University.

Bill and Perleen Oliver . . . . . Dr. William Oliver is the man who perhaps more than any other led the fight against racism in Nova Scotia. He was born in Wolfville, where he was one of the few blacks in the community, and he was the first black graduate of Acadia University. His father and grandfather before him had been superintendents there. Bill

Oliver became a Baptist minister after he got his B.D. (which in this case stands for Bachelor of Divinity!) in 1936. At that time several towns in Pictou County didn't permit blacks to live within their boundaries, and blacks were not permitted burial in Anglican cemeteries in Halifax and Fredericton. After serving in the war as a chaplain, he took over the ministry at Cornwallis Baptist Church in Halifax in addition to his other duties at Beechville, Africville and elsewhere. He was recently honoured by his alma mater and asked to give the convocation address. He died in 1989 about one month before BD. His wife Perleen has always been active in the black community and was born and lived in Africville in Halifax.

Freeman Fennerty . . . . . Baptist minister and church organizer.

Harold Mitton . . . . . pastor Charlottetown and director of Divinity College, Acadia.

Wanda Williams . . . . . bookkeeper, Fredericton.

Reverend Donald Thomas . . . . . pastor, Second Baptist Church, New Glasgow.

Andrew Giffen . . . . . BD's great-grandson.

Introduction

When I first met BD he was 86 and still living in his own home. I had known his son Laurie for some years and he mentioned casually one time that his father had built or renovated over 30 churches in Atlantic Canada. This caught my interest. B.D. Stevens was a contracter, builder and developer of a large part of Halifax over the past 60 years. He began building churches in the middle of his career and was still doing so when he died at 89 in 1989.

BD, as he is unfailingly called, was active in the Baptist Church, but the first church he built was United. He had a strong conviction that communities need churches, and in most cases, with the Baptist Church at least, he devoted as much time to the congregation as to the building. He often bought the land himself or secured the mortgage, and he never charged for his time. Well, that's not true—he sometimes charged one dollar! I would estimate he has given, in time and money, over one million dollars to the Church—or as he would prefer, the Church community, since he saw the Church as people rather than the buildings he made for them. He considered it a good use of his time and money.

BD had an incredibly full life, so that it was as if he lived three lives. I could have chosen a whole different set of anecdotes and stories to describe the man, and I keep hearing new ones all the time! Huge chunks of his story have been left out, including most of his family (he had twenty-eight grandchildren at last count), his second wife and in fact many of his churches. I have only touched on some of his life and tried to give a brief portrait, in his own words and the words of others. But I think the man is here.

It is a "by his works shall ye know him" book. It is not a religious book. BD did not preach; he practiced his faith in a broad sense that goes far beyond the churches he built.

I asked Doris Baker, who was his bookkeeper when he began building churches, if he had had some sort of religious conversion which prompted all this church building. She thought for some time, I'm sure with visions of Billy Graham or Gerry Falwell in her head, and then said, "No. He was always a good man." His story is anecdotal, because that was his style and the way he was with premiers, chief justices, carpenters, or you and me. Imagine this book as a conversation around the kitchen table. He would have liked that.

Peter Brock

Chapter 1
Beginnings

I grew up quite fast.

BD

I was born in 1900, in my grandmother's boarding house in Windsor, Nova Scotia. Twelve years later I went back there as their stable boy. My grandfather Knowles had died and she wanted someone to stay with her, so I went to work at the Windsor Furniture Factory. I did chores night and morning for my board. I used to get up at four in the morning and get things straightened away. Then I went to work at six o'clock and knocked off again at six o'clock at night. I got a dollar a day for it.

From the time I was a kid I always helped whenever there was a chance at woodworking. If they were shingling a barn I would go and help them shingle. Whatever they were doing out in the country I went and helped. But really I didn't lean much to factory work. It was all machinery and they put you on a machine and you stayed there all day feeding lumber in and out again. There wasn't much to learn anymore than hard work.

They had these big kilns they'd put the lumber in to dry. When you wasn't working on the machines, they'd take you into these kilns, and you'd stick the lumber in, piled four ways so the air would go through it. You left it there about two or three weeks, and then you took it out and made furniture out of it. They made a very cheap line of furniture in those days. You could get a chair for $1.25 there.

The people who owned the mill put up a cook house which became a boarding house and my grandmother had bought it. She had money saved up and paid twelve hundred dollars for it. Three stories high and cold as a barn. All the heat they had was from two little coal stoves. The men used to keep the fires going. She used to say, "If you want to keep warm, you've got to look after the fires for me. I can't take the time to look after that, I'm too busy." She had a couple of old fellows, retired men, boarding there and they generally kept the fires going. My grandmother was a great worker. She was a widow woman and would give a good dinner for thirty-five cents. Always had her tables full and everything was home-baked. I was just coming thirteen when I went there.

My father had been left a little farm over in Union Corners. It wasn't very big. He was never a farmer. They pretty near starved to death there, they did. Sometimes my father got work off the farm but mostly there was no work. I used to take them five dollars every Saturday night; used to walk home and take it to them. That had to do until the next week. Five dollars was all they had to live on. That left me a dollar.

It was about nine miles home, over the railroad from Windsor. Sometimes if a fellow was with me I'd take a stick and put it across our shoulders and we'd walk one on one rail, and one on the other. You could walk along right fast that way. I used to try all kinds of things like that.

Laurie Stevens

My dad's father was not a strong individual, but his grandfather was. He used to build ships near Walton, Cheverie and sail them to Boston. They'd build a ship and load her with apples or lumber, depending upon the season, and take her to Boston where they'd sell the cargo, and if they could sell the ship they sold that too. Then they'd come back and build another one. They had a close relationship with the New England-Boston area because of the trade. One time they built what was their biggest ship and my great-grandfather's partner, who was captain, sailed for Boston and never came back. Dad's grandfather blamed himself and just closed down the shipyard and went home. He never opened it again. I guess it just fell apart; they never got a thing out of it after that. It just rotted away. He went home and mourned, for years. My dad's great-uncle built the *Mary Celeste.* They were all close as a family.

BD

The war came on after I was at the furniture factory a year or two. The young fellows were all enlisting in the army and going overseas. They had to lie about their ages to get on. I thought I'd try to get on too. So I went up to the recruiting office, but the fellow knew me. He said "You're not eighteen."

"No, but some of the others are going."

"I don't care about the others; you're not going. But they are hiring people on at the munitions factory over at Trenton, if you want a job. I can get you a job there." I was still getting only $1.00 a day where I was. I remember I went up to Trenton and got $2.85 a day for a start. I thought it was big money.

I paid three dollars a week for room and board at the munitions factory. The places were just like shacks, pretty crude. More women than men worked there. I wasn't full grown but I grew up quite fast. Oh, it was terrible hot in the factory and there were fumes and everything. I didn't like it one bit. One day a fellow came and asked if I would like to cut steel for transport boats they were building, and I told him I'd do anything to get out of the factory. It wasn't more than two days later when I went to work on the boats.

I remember, it was so cold getting those steel sheets up on the side of the boat that we'd pretty near freeze to death. I worked there quite a while. All we did was put steel on the boats. These were transport boats, even carried soldiers, but they were pretty crude. I think there was something like eight hundred men there. We lived in shacks two stories high, and you could look right through them—it was that open. They gave you one blanket, that's all. I used to sleep with my clothes on.

I came to Halifax when I was seventeen, after the explosion. My father came down first after the explosion and no one knew where he was. We never heard from him for a month. They wouldn't let him go home or anything for a while; he had to stay right there and work at the carpentry work. They had thousands of men working there who had never seen a saw in their life. I was a carpenter, and after a while I chanced to get on with them. They were building forty houses off Robie and Almon Street. They were tiny houses and they are still there. They had a bunch of Frenchmen working there, with a man from the Island as superintendent. He saw me working and asked me if I could take a bunch of them and be foreman. I couldn't talk French and I had an awful time trying to speak to them, but anyway we got on after a while. We wouldn't take very long to frame up these little houses and we got teamed up and got going pretty good. They gave me forty men to work with, and they just fell over one another. I'd worked around some and I knew enough about building. My father always did odd jobs for people, and I'd worked with him. He built a couple of barns for different people and I always helped him when I was at home, so I knew what to do. Things changed quite fast in those days. I turned eighteen that spring.

Chapter 2
Heading West

*Your experiences in life will teach
you more than books will.*

BD

After the war they made a big drive for the west, calling for
people to go out and work in the harvest fields. They painted a
great picture of the west in those days. It looked like a place
where you ought to go to get rich quick, or to have a big farm of
your own. A harvest train went out every year, and they were
offering maybe four or five dollars a day, which was way more
than we would get here. So in 1919, I went on the harvest train
that year and headed west. I was nineteen.

The trains had the old tourist cars and those little seats with
slats. That's what you sat on and slept on. We didn't know much.
We took lunch with us, but that only lasted a day or two. It soon
dried up and we couldn't eat it. I was never so hungry in my life.
We didn't have any idea what it would be like. We just thought
we'd get something to eat along the road. We'd stop at a station,
and there'd be a lunch counter selling a bit of stuff, but there
with eight hundred men on that train, if you didn't get there
first you didn't get nothing at all.

We finally stopped at Winnipeg, which was where they hired out of. Farmers said they wanted help, and they'd give you their names and tell you how to look them up when you got to where they were. We went to Granville, Alberta, and when we got there, a fellow was waiting at the station for us. He took us on. We had nowhere to sleep, so they let us use the hayloft in the stable.

A fellow by the name of Haddon Swinamer came with us. He shook all the time so we called him Shaky. He was about forty-five. No one wanted to hire him at all, but we said, "Take him on and try him. He's a great worker." Well, he had never used horses. They had oxen out Chester Road, where he came from. Next morning, just about the break of day, we saw old Swinamer jumping over these raised wooden sidewalks they had out there, falling over the hitching posts. He was like a wild man. "Haddon, what's wrong?" I asked. "Oh, I can't work out here; they give me these horses."

They told him to harness the horses, so he took the collar and stuck it up in front of the horse, thinking the horse was going to stick his head into it, the way oxen do. Well, the horse flew out backwards, tore his rope off and was away. That happened to two or three of them.

They told poor old Haddon he was no good and to get back home again. He came to me, and do you know, he hadn't a cent with him. We gave him a dollar or two, and interceded at the station to get him a pass home. He was nine or ten days getting home, and he had only a little bit to eat all the way. However he stood that, I don't know.

They had no bunk house for us, so we took a wagon and built a bunk out of it and covered it with straw so we'd have something to sleep in. There were snakes and everything in it. It was terrible.

The fellow who'd hired us said, "I'd like to build a barn. I have some plans here. Do you think you could build me a barn? Just a small barn, one of those round roofed ones."

"Well, I guess so," I said. We got the stuff, and another fellow helped me build it. He was working for a friend down the road, and later the friend came and got us to build one for him. So I built two barns that fall. It got so cold, I had a hard job shingling it or doing anything to the second one. It was down to forty below zero, but we worked away and got it done.

That fall we took the job of looking after the two ranches. Jennsen, the fellow I was working for, said, "Now, I'm going to Winnipeg, and I'll send you feeder cattle and you look after them and feed them. When spring comes, we'll share the money we make on them." Here I was, a bachelor out there in a shack all alone with these cattle. We had a lot of cows in calf, and when they started to have calves, they were freezing to death out in the cold. So I went to work and built what they call a strawbarn. You build two walls of poles, and you take the threshing machine and blow straw between them. And then you put up rafters and blow straw on top of them. That makes a barn. It's surprisingly warm inside there. We put the cattle that were going to calve in there, and it saved the calves. I had quite a few calves that spring.

The next fall we did some changing around. We each bought a quarter section of land. A fellow named McPhee from Noel, near home, opened up a lumber yard, and he used to take horses in trade for lumber. He owned the place and must have had five hundred horses or more around there. McPhee told us that for every horse we broke for him, he'd give us one for ourselves. So we started breaking horses every chance we'd get. McPhee turned round and sold quite a number we had broken for him. So long as you could drive them away, they'd pay for them. Soon I had seventeen and my friend Keith had eighteen. We hadn't bothered breaking ours; they were still wild.

This was lovely land in that part of the country. You have to plow the year before you're going to sow, so that fall we kept working for the boss. There were quite a few farms not being worked, so he rented them, went to the bank and borrowed the money and bought seed. Then he bought two tractors, one for each of us. We worked from daylight to dusk on those farms, putting in crop. It came up about two feet or so, just as green and strong as you'd want to see. And then there came a chinook wind

15

and it was all just flattened and blown away. He lost everything he had. He owed us both eight hundred dollars in back wages but he was a pretty straight fellow. He said, "You fellows worked hard here. I'm going to lose everything anyway. I'll go down to the bank while I can still get the money." He got sixteen hundred dollars and paid each of us. He said goodbye, and away we went. We just let our horses go.

We thought we'd go through to the coast and work in the woods there, because we had worked in the woods back home. We got through to British Columbia and took their log train back to the woods. They had big camps, and the fellow there could see we knew nothing about their kind of logging. We said to him, "Any chance of getting on?"

He said,"Well, there's a fellow killed here about every half day; you can get a job topping if you want to."

These fellows would climb to the top of the tree, and if the wind blew it took the top off and them with it, and they'd be gone. We looked at one another and said we guessed we had better get home.

We each had a little bag with a blanket in it. These log trains carried massive logs, sixty to eighty feet long. We rode one out for about eighty miles. You had to hang on all the time. By the time we got there we were so stiff we could hardly get off the thing. We didn't know what to do from there.

We still had our money sewed inside our shirts; we hadn't spent any. So we decided to get back to the prairie area, where we knew we could get work. So we hopped a freight train and rode in the freight car with about a dozen other hobos. As soon as we came on board they wanted to know all about us and whether we had any money to buy them some food. Some of them were half starved to death. Once we got on we couldn't get off again until the train stopped. Night came, and we sat back-to-back. We never slept, I don't think. You daren't sleep for fear of being robbed.

We stopped at Red Deer first, and then Moose Jaw, where we got off and got jobs with Glennies, which was a big firm with elevators all over the west, and they had farms along with them.

We got work with these Glennies putting in crop. Stayed with their foreman and his family—Morris was their name—and we found them very nice people. We stayed until after Christmas and then decided to come home. We were going to stay all winter but decided we wouldn't, so we had to pay full fare to get back.

We didn't get rich in the west or buy a big farm. We left the quarter section and let all the horses go—turned them loose on the prairie. I was twenty-one when I came home.

Before I went West, I wouldn't have tried a lot of things that I did when I came back. I grew up quite a bit. The fellows I worked for taught me a lot about taking chances. They would buy land, put a big crop in and then lose everything. Still they went on just the same the next year. Your experiences in life will teach you more than books will. It started me thinking bigger.

Elizabeth Knowles, BD's grandmother,
who owned a rooming house in Windsor.

Students of the "Little Red School House." BD is second from
the right in the back row.

Walter Salter, BD, and his brother Bill out west in 1919.

BD's parents.

Chapter 3
Starting Business

*I always found I could do things
better on my own than if someone
was bossing me.*

Laurie Stevens

My dad was brought up in a very frugal, very simple household manner and community. Most of the people did not have much of an intellectual education. They were mostly physical people, and they needed direction. So anybody who would take the leadership role in those days, he won his position quickly. They'd say, "Ask him, he'll tell us what to do."

It was that way particularly in the lumber woods. So many of those men looked for direction, and they'd do anything in the world, but somebody had to direct them. I was just a kid, but I could see it. Some of them were big and brawny, but they weren't stupid. They weren't about to make decisions, but if somebody else made one they'd carry it out. And they'd try hard to make sure they carried it out to the best of their ability. It was amazing to watch them because they were not stupid; they just had never been challenged to make decisions about what to do next. You might think the guys couldn't think on their own, but it wasn't that. It was just that all their life they'd done it that way.

My dad was the oldest in a family of eight, and decisions came easy to him. He decided quickly what had to be done, and I've seen him snap people around like I-don't-know-what; they'd just jump and run and do things. I always used to think it's a wonder they don't get mad and say, "I'm not going to do that." But they always respected him. It was even that way when he went west at nineteen. They were all the same age, but he had been working for five years, and the other guys hadn't, so he just naturally became the leader.

BD

I went home to the family farm and put in a garden, but I didn't stay around long. I went out to work at whatever I could get, but there was not a lot available. I decided to go to the States and ended up in Bristol, Connecticut, working in a barrel factory. I didn't like that one little bit and spent the evenings looking for something else. After a couple of weeks I found a fellow who was building tenement houses, and I was hired as foreman at sixty dollars a week—big money in those days. But there was a girl back home.

Laurie Stevens

Her family came from Martock. There were three girls and two boys. They were hardworking people, farmers—and tough. Dad's first job was nearby at Windsor, so I presume they knew each other for a long time before they were married.

BD

Eva Redden was living at home looking after her mother, and she didn't want to go to the States. We decided to marry. I left my tools in Connecticut and promised to return—one of the few promises I guess I didn't keep. We were married six months later.

Helen Thompson

My mother's family lived on the farm in Martock. Her father died very young. Then her mother was washing the floor one day and drove a needle in her hand and had to have her arm cut off up to the elbow. My mother had to take over, so she and her brother ran the farm. Her mother decided if she had a leather cup on her arm, she could bring in money by quilting. So this is what she did. She made quilts and she could do a lot of things in the house. Her mother brought their family up by not looking at other people's faults. And she was a great woman. If you'd said, "Oh, they're no good," she'd say, "What's wrong with them. Don't you have that same fault in another way?" There was never anybody that had any faults. They had a right to live their life.

My father went with her younger sister for a long time, and then she went off and married another man. So he didn't know my mother for long, though they knew one another. They just went together for a short while before they were married. He had to look after his family and she knew that, so they both had a lot in common that way.

BD

We lived in Windsor after we got married. I was working in the woods and bringing in about thirty dollars a month. I bought a piece of land for one hundred dollars at Currie's Corner and began to build my own home, working nights and whenever I could. Below the house was a railway siding and they'd been shipping lumber there all winter. They culled it pretty sharp and put the culls on one side—must have had about 150,000 board feet piled there. The man piling it asked me if I wanted to buy it. I said I couldn't; I had no money except for $178.00 for payment on my house. I asked my wife and she said, "No, don't buy it. You don't need it, and dear knows when you'd ever sell it." We had a mortgage on our house at Windsor. I had some money in the bank for the mortgage but was wondering whether we were going to make it or not. The bank manager said they would foreclose if I missed the house payment. I thought it over a lot. I knew I shouldn't do it, but anyway, I went ahead and bought the lumber.

Two weeks later I was sitting in the yard when a fellow I knew well came along. He said, "I wonder who owns this lumber? We need some for the road in the woods." I told him I did and sold some to him for over eight hundred dollars. He tallied it himself. What he took didn't make a hole in it at all. I guess I eventually made about three thousand dollars; it really put me on my feet. Every time I sold lumber I took one tenth of the money with me to the church. That was the start of my tithing. My wife was a strong believer in tithing as well.

Over the years, I oftentimes found that after I'd paid the men Friday night I would end up without enough left to get our groceries. But I figured that the church had to go on as well, and just because I'd made a mess of it and hadn't made enough money was no reason why I shouldn't be giving, even if I had to borrow to do it. I felt there was no harm in that.

A local farmer was building a new home and asked me to help. In a sense that was the beginning of my building. It was noised around that I was a good builder, and soon I had all the work I could handle. Soon I had five houses on the go, working with my brother and one other man. Other than the lathing, we did all the work. For the inside finishing, we had the Windsor Furniture Factory, where I had begun working at twelve years of age, make the casings and baseboards from wood we brought to their kiln.

At that time, a cousin, Reg Hart, wanted me to come to Halifax to put up a large building for him—a meal mill. He said he would give me a lot more than I was getting in Windsor. So I went down to Halifax and started in there. First I had to take down an old coal shed. It was all framed in sixty-foot lengths of eight-by-sixteen hard pine or Douglas Fir. They were dried so hard that when we dropped them from about seventy feet, they just bounced like a ball. We took them to Barrett's Mill to get them sawed into planks. Harold Barrett said the saw turned blue they were so hard and that they couldn't saw them. I said we should put them in the pond. Well, they shoved them in for two weeks, and the saw went right through them after that.

I worked with Hart for about a year and built the meal mill. Then he wanted me to build five ice-cream truck bodies. He

23

wanted them built right on truck chassis, insulated with cork, and he wanted them as strong and light as they could be.

I always found I could do things a lot better on my own than if someone was bossing me. I told Hart that I would like to go on my own. I'd take the job of building the trucks, but on my own. The average carpenter's wage was about twenty-four dollars a week and me and my brother were making sixty, which was good wages... But I had always been a freelancer.

Hart said, "You're awful foolish. You will never make that much on your own." Well, I didn't at first. We had hard scratching for a year or two, but I made a lot more than that after a while. So we broke clear and went to work on the truck bodies. We built the first one in four or five days and I charged eight hundred dollars for it. Hart said, "I can't pay you eight hundred dollars for that, there's only about two hundred dollars labour into it." I told him we had worked almost night and day, and I figured we were giving him a good deal. It would have cost over three thousand dollars to build in the factory. So I told him to forget it; we could get along without that work. He came back after trying it out himself and asked us to build five more so we agreed—at the same price. We were doing all right. In those days sixty dollars a week was big pay, and we were making three hundred a week building them.

For a while after that we were doing mostly repair work but it got around that we did good work and we began to build houses. At first we did it all on cost plus because we couldn't afford to take a contract. We paid for materials as we went along. Every cent we got went into lumber.

Art Smith

I remember him in those days, riding a bicycle with a saw strapped onto the handle bars and a toolbox on the back. He used to go to Windsor to see his wife on the weekends, which was just Sundays. BD's brother had come to Halifax to work with him, and they bought lots, side-by-side, in what is now Fairview, to build their new homes. They worked on them nights mostly. BD built a garage first and lived in that while he built the house.

BD

We had quite a little family by the time we moved down to Halifax. My wife and five children lived in the garage. I often think of what my wife went through, what we went through. We went through it together. She was a wonderful person. It was crowded, and it was cold. If you stayed close to the stove you could stay warm. When night came, you just covered up with more blankets.

Next door was Art Roma; he was a bootlegger on the side. People would go there and get drunk; they'd even come pounding on our door. I said to Roma, "My wife is scared to stay here nights when these people come round. If it keeps on I'm not going to report you to the police; I'm going to come over and punch the stuffings out of you." He was a good neighbour after that. When people got drunk, he would put them into an old motorcycle sidecar and dump them down the road somewheres.

There were lots of bootleggers in those days. I guess it was pretty vicious sometimes. There was all kinds of stuff into it. He just put in enough whiskey or brandy or whatever to flavour it good.

Helen Thompson

He was a nice man, but Dad never saw that because he was away a lot. Weekends was the time for them to bring in their store of stuff, to hide it. Us kids all had to go to the bathroom at the same time because the bathroom window was on that side of the house. Poor Mr. Roma would be hiding his stuff in a flooded basement. We'd all get up in the bathroom window and watch him put the bottles in the bags and dip them down in the water.
Poor Dad, he could never understand that one. He'd say, "Why do those girls all have to get in that bathroom at the same time?" And my mother would say, "That's all right, Burnett. You can

have it soon. Once they all come out, they won't want to go in there again." She knew what was going on because she was great friends of Mrs. Roma. Of course, Mum never saw anything she didn't want to see. Dad had the Mounties out one time later and they came to the door and Mum said, "I don't know what Burnett is talking about. We don't have nothing like that around here." So they left. She always said, "That's those people—we're living together—and that's what they're doing. You don't have to do it."

BD

My wife kept my books. She had the accounts all set up but had never even taken bookkeeping in school. I remember the auditor saying, "Good gracious, you'd think that woman had gone to college or something the way she writes things up." Everything was right in order.

I got involved helping to build a little church at Fairview. I was always interested in seeing the church go ahead. There were four of us and we thought of starting a Baptist church and we really went at it. Boss Hubley was in concrete, and he poured the foundation for us. I had lumber on hand, some, and I gradually bought a little more to go with it. My brother Bill was with us. It was not a big church, but it took a lot of effort at the time. We couldn't get a minister, so they sent us students from the United College at Dalhousie. It wasn't long before we began to draw quite a lot of people. There was only four or five Baptists, yet we built the church. The rest were United so it became a United Church.

After a while they sent us a retired minister, Dr. Rackham. He was just a little man but, oh, he was as witty and comical as could be. He'd keep a whole crowd laughing over almost nothing, just seeing the funny side of things. He said prayer was the strength of the Church. "If I can get all of you praying we'll have a strong church. If you can't talk to the Lord there's no way of getting along with each other."

My brother became United and is still. Later he helped to build a United church on Dutch Village Road, and he and his family all moved there. The original church is now called something like "Independent Baptist." I can hardly remember; I haven't been in it for over forty years.

Laurie Stevens

I was just a kid when the second war was on. I remember one time Dad wanted to buy a truck, so we went down to New Ross to look at an International. It was a snowy night, and the owner, Mr. Meisner, said, "Well, I'm not taking a cheque. No, sir. I've got a truck and if you want it I'll sell it to you, but it's got to be cash." Dad talked him into driving into Halifax and staying the night with us. He said he'd get him the cash, and drive him back the next day. That night the three of us got into Fairview at about nine o'clock at night. We pulled that big International truck into the yard and Meisner said, "Well, where are you going to get the money this time of night?"

We drove over to Kempt Road where Levi Boyd lived. It was snowing hard. We drove up to the house and knocked on the door. No answer. Then Dad opened the window and stuck his head in and yelled, "Levi, it's Burnie Stevens." A voice came back saying, "God, have you started drinkin'?"

"No, I need some money. I'm trying to buy a truck."

"Dear God, it's ten o'clock at night." Levi threw his pants down and said, "The money's in the pocket. Take out what you need and give me the rest back tomorrow."

My dad took the pants, took the money out, paid Meisner $1,100 for the truck, and took the rest of the money home. The next morning Dad went back to Levi to give him back his money back. He said, "I took $1,100 and here's the rest."

"How much is there now?"

"$3,100."

"Jeeze, that's $300 more than I thought I had. I should lend you money more often."

That's the way those guys carried on. They always had an elastic band around a bunch of bills. They grew up that way and they completely trusted one another. If they trusted you, they trusted you. If they didn't, they wouldn't give you the time of

27

day. Levi used to be in the coal business, and at the end of the week he'd come over with his roll and say, "Count it for me; you're better at counting than I am." They used to trade stuff back and forth. If they were making a deal they'd fight all day over one hundred dollars but if they were giving you money, well, that was a different thing. They didn't have too much education, and they only had one thing to rely on—their honesty. They had to have their integrity or there would be nothing left.

In 1941 or so, Dad had a sort of heart attack, and the doctor told him he should get out of the city and relax. So he bought a farm up at West Gore and was going to go farming. He had been brought up on a farm. To begin with he had to clear most of the land, and in clearing the land he set up a mill. Well, he got so involved in the lumber business that he never did go farming. I lived in the woods with him and I used to travel with him, and in the winter he would park the car and walk for five miles to get into the woods camp. He used to work day and night. Gosh, he was always on the move.

His first mill was in West Gore, which was a rented mill. Then he bought one from Gordon Isnor which burned down the day he bought it. We drove up in a little half-ton truck, and the mill was in a shambles. Later he had a mill in Hammonds Plains, and another at Hardwoodlands, but the biggest was at Shubie on the St. Andrews River, behind the game farm.

BD

I bought that mill from Gordon Isnor up in Lantz, and then lent it to him to finish out a cut he was doing. There was no insurance on it when it burned down. He said, "Well, you loaned it to me, and I'll try to replace it the best I can." He did, but it wasn't as good as the mill that had burned.

Most of the lumber was being sold overseas at good prices, so I bought land up on Hammonds Plains Road and sawed there for three years selling to the government for use overseas. I just had a wartime license and the year the war ended they took the license away from me. By then I had put another small mill in and had about 3 million board feet on hand, which I would have got $130 a thousand for on the overseas market. Local markets were only paying about $54 a thousand, so I pretty near went out of business. I had to sell twelve homes I had, to pay my bills. I was the only one up there to pay all his bills—the rest just bailed out and left.

Laurie Stevens

Charlie McCulloch was politically involved and he was the only one who had his export license renewed after the war. The only other fellow who had a license was George Lordly, who was sort of the dean of export lumber in Nova Scotia. So all the lumber that was to be exported had to be sold to those two fellows. My dad and everybody had been exporting overseas during the war and getting good prices when all of a sudden— bang. Of course my dad got so mad he wouldn't sell to McCulloch. He would only sell to Lordly.

About 1945 or '46 he packed it in. That year he got so mad he brought all his lumber home. We lived on Main Avenue, and there was a yard behind the house. He must have had 200,000 feet of lumber there. I worked there "sticking" it, and he used it later to build houses.

Fairview Community United Church.

Chapter 4
Contracting

*I came into this world without anything,
so I figured I couldn't lose very much.*

Laurie Stevens

Dad lost a lot of money over the years. He'd lose and start again—somewhere he'd find a way to start again. He always had great faith in starting again.

Blair Williams

BD told me that when he came out of the woods he had two hundred dollars. That's where he started from after the lumber went sour; it was something like the crash in the stock market. He told me he sold off everything: tractor, horses, mills, everything.

He then found some land out on Bayers Road and went to a banker and said he needed so much money by the following Friday. I guess they weren't going to let him have it but somehow he bought it anyway and the next year he sold off some of it for the shopping centre, and that's how he started again. He told the banker that streetcars would be running out there in two years, and they were. Well, maybe it's not as simple as that.

BD

It took quite a little while before I was established enough to go ahead on my own and keep a crowd of men on again after the lumbering went. I went with Eastern Trust, which is now Central Trust and after a while they got enough confidence in me so I could get loans. It took quite a bit of negotiating at first, but later, whatever I brought to them they never turned down. But I had to take some wild chances.

Old Harry Deal owned twenty acres on Bayers Road. He had some cows and the like but had stopped farming. He was pretty old then and deaf as a doornail. I went to him and told him I was looking for land for a church. He said, "Well, gracious man ... you don't need no more churches—they're only half full now." Anyway he wanted $20,000 for his twenty acres and I told him I'd give him $1,000 now and the rest when he got the deed ready. He said, "Aren't you going to beat me down or anything?"

"No, you seem to be a man who expects to get his price."

"Well now, the Lord will be with you, whatever you do."

I bought his land around Bayers Road for $20,000. Then I broke it up into lots and put in sewer and water. It was worth $200,000 in just a year. It was a matter of seeing where a bit of land was going to be valuable before long. You had to improve it, that's the thing. But the biggest trouble was getting the money to buy it in the first place. The banks would only let me have so much.

After I got the deed, I told him I had given four lots to the church. He thought I was crazy. Later an oil company came to ask if they could buy those lots for a service station and offered me forty thousand dollars. I said I had already given them to the church and couldn't take them back. They bought land across the road and there is a gas station there now.

I had tried to buy that whole piece there where the Bayers Road Shopping Centre is now. I went to the bank but they wouldn't lend me the money. Only a few days later Sammy Butler bought the whole thing for $27,000. He was a shrewd old fellow. Later, he sold off a few lots to Dominion Stores for $105,000 and later a lot on the corner to the oil company for

$40,000. But I couldn't finance it myself. I offered $25,000, and they would have taken that, but the bank wouldn't go for it. That was the equivalent of about $200,000 now, and it looked like an awful big loan. They said I already had enough land and that I should develop what I had.

I went ahead and built houses on the rest of what I had. I put in water, sewer, streets, everything. The city wasn't going to do it, so I borrowed the money from the bank and went ahead. The houses sat there all summer and didn't move, so I decided to sell them myself. I always thought that you needed an agent to sell them, but I discovered that the agents didn't know how to finance them. One fellow came and wanted to buy but couldn't find the down payment. "Well," I said, "I'll go to the bank and borrow the money for you and you can give me a note for it, and we can mortgage the rest." It wasn't two or three days before he brought a friend who wanted to do the same thing. That's the way we sold all those houses. The idea was so new, I never let anyone know what we were doing. If we had, the banks wouldn't have loaned me the money. I did the same later on with twenty-two homes up at Bridgeview one spring.

I took the biggest chances when I developed Bridgeview subdivision. I put three hundred thousand dollars into it before I took out even a dollar. That's as good as three million today. I had to buy an apartment building and tear it down to get the road in, and I had to move three other houses and give them new ones in exchange, though I later moved and sold the old ones.

The biggest job is getting other people to realize you are on the right track. I had to put a water line out to Bridgeview from Fairview too. I dug ten wells and couldn't get hardly any water at all, not enough for a subdivision. At the time, I was also building houses in the city and I was involved with Mulgrave Park Church. Everyone thought I was crazy. I used to say I never worried a great deal, but I was concerned sometimes.

Blair Williams.

We had an awful problem getting water. Someone told BD that if you put dynamite down a well that you could sometimes get water. So they loaded it up during the daytime and ran a wire up through the bushes to the road. They knew it was going to make quite a smash, so they crept in at night and set her off. Well, the blast certainly shook the hill. At the time there were several of those planes around—Avengers—and a couple of them had crashed recently. People thought it was either a bomb or a plane crash. BD kept it pretty quiet for a few days. It was about three weeks before it leaked out that they had blown the well. He didn't get any water, though.

BD

I gave up and went to the Public Service Commission and asked them to give me a figure on what a water line would cost. It was so high that I couldn't afford to pay it, so I asked them, if I put the line in, would they take it over? They said, "If you put it in to our specifications and have our inspectors look at it, that would be agreeable." So I put a note in the bank for $300,000 and arranged for them to collect $100 from each house I put in. They were better able to collect it than me, because they could shut off the water.

A fellow named Carson Staples dug the whole thing. He still works with us. We rented a backhoe for $500 to do the job. There wasn't hardly a night that Carson wouldn't spend fixing it and keeping it repaired. When we were through with it, we never even bothered to haul it away; it was almost gone. Someone got it for scrap. He dug the whole place out with that old backhoe and made money on the deal. We did it for one-third what the Public Service had quoted. Today it would cost two million. So that's how the main got put in to Bridgeview. It's the same water they're all using there now, and the water they're using in Rockingham too.

Wayne Langley

I started working for BD when I was in grade ten—the summer of 1952. He payed me thirty-five cents an hour as a carpenter's assistant. By the end of the summer, I got a big increase to fifty cents. I got on regular pick and shovel work the second summer. I went on working for five or six summers.

We would use very basic equipment, like handmade winches and lifting stuff. One day I got wiped out in the ditch when a winch broke. We should have been using a much stronger device. And we used to carry a lot of heavy steel beams, and pipes. We'd get six, eight, ten men and get the beams up on our shoulders and lug them. For supplies, he would ask a few questions, say, "Uhuh, uhuh," and then say, "Well, your going to need this much"—just like that—and what we needed was always available.

He expected people to treat him as he treated them, that is very honestly, very sincerely. He could also give you a good hard stare if he thought that what he was hearing wasn't all the facts. He'd always stand and look at you and really forced you to let things out and to be very forthright about it. He was very effective that way. He didn't sound off, but he could sure make a point.

Blair Williams

One winter, we were building some houses and a basement drifted in with snow, about three feet deep, even though we had a roof on. We put a ladder down into the snow in the stairwell. BD was a big man, and Harry Rockwell, one of the foremen, was also a big man. Harry went down first, and when BD stepped on the top of the ladder of course both their weights on made it sink down into the snow. BD fell on top of poor old Harry, and I heard them hollering. It was an odd-looking sight, both of them laying in the snow laughing. They couldn't get up. Harry was underneath and BD on top, with his feet up through the ladder. I went down and got them on their feet. BD said something very funny. They could have been hurt, but he joked it off pretty good.

BD

There were quite a few small contractors here, and things were beginning to move ahead quite a little bit. I still had an old secondhand half-ton. Some of these contractors came to work all dressed up, and they wouldn't think of putting on a nail apron and helping the men. Some of them said I was working just like a labourer, night and day, "Why don't you just sit back, hire a foreman, and make some money, take it easy," they said.

I didn't want to start branching out, getting a big office. I had an office under my house. If I got a chance at all, I dug in just the same as the rest of the men. I'd put a nail apron on and go to work laying out studs, or shingling. I used to just love to shingle, especially if we got good western cedar. The men would appreciate it if you worked with them. One fellow said the reason they worked so hard was because they had to to keep up with me. He said they'd be ashamed of what they were doing and go at it harder than ever. I always felt I had to carry my end with the men. It means a lot to them.

Blair Williams

He had an awful knack for splitting rock. When we were pouring doorsteps for the houses we were building at Bridgeview, we put a lot of rock in to save concrete. We had a bunch ready and one day, BD came along and got out and started breaking rock. He split them, about the same as you would split wood, and we carried them and piled them. He worked right along with us from house to house. He loved to do that kind of thing.

Andrew Levy

I had been working for the CN. The work was over and I picked up my U.I.C. book and was on my way home for dinner. BD stopped me in the street. "Are you working?"

"No, I just finished at the railway."

"Do you want to come to work for me?"

"Yes."

"When can you start? This afternoon?"

"All right. Well, come right down here," and he pointed down Rowe Avenue. So I started in that afternoon stripping forms.

I had met BD at church at Mulgrave Park, which was his first big adventure, and I knew he was in the housebuilding business but that was all. It was not like working for a boss but more like for a friend. Sometimes he would come to my house on a Saturday.

"Not working today, Andrew?"

"No. Well come on down, I'll give you something to do."

That summer BD had something like forty men working for him, and he had no foreman. I don't know of a man among them who had a complaint or a grumble. We'd meet at seven-thirty, and he'd come into the shack and say to one of the men, "What do you plan to do today…? OK, and what do you plan to do?"

"Well, I'm working with so and so."

"Great, great."

We'd go and be ready to hammer at eight. We'd quit for lunch at exactly noon and go back right at twelve-thirty and work to four-thirty. No stopping at four-fifteen to pick up your tools. We had twenty-three or twenty-four houses to build that summer, and it went like wildfire. He would come round to see if we had everything we needed, help with problems. One time he saw a carpenter take his level and put it on a stud, and then put it back in his toolbox. BD took a hammer and drove a nail into the stud and hung the level on it. He said, "You see that, it's there when you need it." He'd see things quick as a flash and help you to do a better job. Another time I remember, he saw a man hanging doors, putting the screws in with a screwdriver. BD said, "Gracious man, that's too slow. Those slots are just for taking them out. Use a hammer." He always saw what you were doing, but mostly it was like working on your own.

One day he drew me aside and said, "I'm going to give you a little raise; I hope you won't be mad at me." I had only been with him a couple of weeks. He kept it all in his head, and he trusted everyone. It was amazing.

Another Saturday, we were out at Bedford putting a roof on a church when BD came round, at about a quarter to four. He wanted the job finished that day so the roofer could start the next week. He would always put on a nail apron like the other men, and sometimes it was quite comical because he'd be working away and no one would know who he was. Anyway we were all there and he said, "Andrew, I'll saw and you hammer," and he took to cutting.

I said, "There is a horse over there if you want it. "

"Well," he said, "I had a knee before I had a horse," and he just kept cutting away. Five o'clock came, and when we hadn't finished he asked a couple of us to come back after supper to finish off. We never thought of not doing it. That's the way it was working with BD. Winter was coming on. I was asked to go back to the railway, and I was expecting to get laid off with BD. But he came to me and said, "I want to loan you to the heating contractor for a couple of weeks. He wants you to cut holes and the like of that." Here I was expecting to get laid off and instead I went to work with the heating contractor. After a couple of weeks I was named foreman, and I worked with the heating contractor for six and one half years. We did all BD's work.

Blair Williams

BD was very loyal to people who worked for him, and they were to him. The MacDonalds used to do roofing, and they would drop the job they were doing and go to BD if he wanted them. They knew he was going to pay them right off. A lot of people would do his work ahead of somebody else's because they knew when they were done he would pay them. They wouldn't have to wait for their money. For furnaces, later it was Andrew Levy, for plastering it was Lawrence Herbert, and for any roofing he got the MacDonalds.

He didn't shop around for prices. He'd call them up and say, "I've got a roof, come and do it," and he expected them not to soak him. But he knew when he was being used, right? One time he had a fellow doing some dozer work for him, and he had a backhoe there, too. BD was paying so much for each machine every day. He came one morning to see if they were getting the work done, and found they had only one operator for two machines. You didn't pull that with BD for long and you didn't get work after if you tried it. He didn't go flying at him. He paid what he owed him: "Get your bill made out now and we'll settle up." But there wasn't a next time.

Andrew Levy

He was always full of fun. He got a new Dodge truck one time and was taking a big fellow who worked for him to a new job. The fellow said what a fine truck it was. "Oh yes," said BD, "you can even shut off the motor and it will keep running." The truck had a noisy heater, and he shut the heater off and the truck kept going.

BD

I used to get into a lot of trouble one way or another. I had trouble with unions and inspectors and the like. One time I wanted to build a motel, the Wedgwood. I had bought the lot for two thousand dollars and took a hill from across the road to fill it in with rock. We had three or four big trucks moving rock, and they came to complain about us stopping traffic. Then they wouldn't give us a permit—said we didn't have a good bottom. They sent the inspector out several times, and the men were afraid that he would stop the job. I went down and threw him off the lot. You couldn't prove it wasn't a good bottom. We built the motel on a slab, one of the first here, and it is standing today. If I'd listened to them, we wouldn't have a motel there now. When I had a job to do, I generally went ahead and did it, with or without a permit. But I generally made sure I had a good lawyer.

The unions are a hard bunch to fight. I had ten houses started over behind Bridgeview, and things were going well when the union stepped in. I didn't recognize the union, but the plumbers and electricians were all union. Our fellows were making more than union rates. We didn't pay overtime, but I was giving my foremen an extra hour's pay a day, and we were also working a lot of hours. I had work for them pretty near all the time. A lot of fellows who belonged to the union couldn't get work enough to keep them going. And I was bringing in carpenters from out of town because I couldn't get good men here.

They shut us down, and it was six months before we got it straightened away. We had forty men hired on. I took work out of town to try to keep my men going, but couldn't keep it up. I had quite a lot of money tied up at the time. I had bought the land and put in streets, water and sewer.

Blair Williams

Back when we first started building houses we used to work Saturdays for straight time. Ol' BD, lots of Saturdays, he'd roll in along about a half-hour before quitting time, and he'd go around and pass out twenty-dollar bills to all the men. That was a lot of money back in those days, but he knew they'd earned it. "Here's a little extra for you to buy something," he'd say. Not many fellows would do that. But he knew when a man had done a good day's work.

BD

All the time I was selling houses and borrowing for the people, for their down payment, I never had one go back on me. But one time I bought a piece of land in Dartmouth —something like 30 lots—and the city wouldn't put water into it, so again I did it myself. I put the water in across my piece to a subdivision that Charlie McCulloch was developing. They hooked right onto it and kept on going. It cost about $12,000 and they were to pay half. A lot of the time I just took a man's word for whatever he told me, but it doesn't take many times like that before you're careful. I didn't take his anymore. I never trusted them after that and shouldn't have then, after what he did to us in the lumber business.

When we got through with Bridgeview we had about 425 lots. When we started selling the lots were $800, and at the last they were selling for about $4,500. We developed over a million dollars worth of land there. I always liked to build houses for people. That's what Bridgeview was—just plain houses. But sometimes you had to take what looked like heavy chances. It's all part of your life. When you get into it, it's like a disease, just one thing after another: you see a piece of land somewhere and figure if you could get it and develop it... I came into this world without anything, so I figured I couldn't lose very much.

Chapter 5
Mulgrave Park

*You'll never have anything unless
you give it away.*

BD

I've had a lot of dealings with banks and I can say they're scared to death of churches. They daren't take a lien against a church: they'd never get their money. There's nobody to sue. This was what happened when I needed a loan for the Mulgrave Park Church. Ten men from West End Church in Halifax said they would go on notes to the bank to raise enough money to start with—one thousand dollars apiece. I gave them the deed so they could get the money. But then we had a meeting and they weren't sure whether they should do that or not: they felt if some of the fellows died off they'd all be responsible for the money, and they got frightened and backed out. So I got up and said that if they'd give me back the deed I'd borrow the money and build the church on my own. They gave it back, and I went down to the bank and borrowed five thousand dollars. That's all they would lend me in those days. Those bank managers were scared to even lend me that much. We put up the basement first, and they started to worship in that.

The bank manager soon got after me. He was a sharp little fellow. He said, "Those people up there haven't paid a cent since you took the loan."

I said, "Are you afraid of it?"

"Well, yes," he said. "It doesn't look good on my books and I'll have to do something about it."

"All right," I said. "I think I have enough in my account; just charge it up to me."

"I don't want to do that," he said.

"Well, that's the only way you'll get paid and I'll likely have to pay it in the end anyway." Those were the days when you had to scratch for a dollar, I'll tell you.

In the meantime, I was well acquainted with the Superintendent of the Baptist Convention and he came to see me and wanted to know how we got started. So I told him the story and he said, "Well, I'll get you some money." He sent me $2,500, and I put that right in the bank.

Then Harvey Denton who was the minister of the First Baptist Church had $1,500 from an outreach program and he said, "I'll give you that." Then the West End Church sent me $1,000 so I paid off my loan and we got started building again.

By the time we were ready to build the church, it had grown a lot. Harry Renfree was the first minister there. He built the church, the congregation, by going from door to door. At first they thought he was Jehovah's Witness and the kicked him out. He was very persistent, and he built the congregation just by meeting people. He used to have get-togethers at night, and potluck suppers. Got a few every time. Oh, he was a wonderful fellow.

Harry Renfree

I first met BD Stevens while I was still a student at Acadia University, in 1950. At the same time I was also a pastor of the Gaspereau, White Rock, and Melanson group of churches. He came to the parsonage in Gaspereau with the Reverend Athol Roberts, who is now, interestingly enough, a medical doctor and president of the Canadian Medical Association. He came to ask me to become pastor of the newly established Mulgrave Park Church in Halifax. I really hesitated because I still had a year to go on my divinity degree. However, he was so persuasive that my wife Rose and I, with our three sons, moved to Halifax in the fall of 1950 and took up our task. We had an understanding that I would be able to complete my year at Pine Hill Divinity Hall of the United Church of Canada, which I did.

When we arrived in Halifax, Mulgrave Park was in its early stages, with thirty members and a rather simple basement building. But already they had in mind to put an upper floor on it, which of course they did and that is now the church hall.

BD

L.E. Shaw, who was a great worker for the church, heard about the Sunday school we had started. We had so many children coming to the school we didn't know what to do with them—the church basement wasn't nearly big enough. So I brought him there one day, and it was so unruly that day you could hardly hear the teacher. "Hell, look Stevens," he said, "go down to our yard and if there is anything there you can use to put on some extra rooms, take it."

I said, "We could use some concrete blocks."

"Well, just go and get what you need. I'll send an order down."

So we went and got bricks and mortar, and we put five classrooms up. That started us going again. There were people giving money— small amounts, fifty dollars or so—all the time, and by the time we had the classrooms done they were all paid for and we were starting to raise money for the church.

Harry Renfree

I remember soon after we arrived in Halifax, BD was building some twenty houses. I went over to see him one night, and the phone was just about ringing off the hook, and so in desperation I actually stuffed the phone in one of the drawers of his desk. He let me get away with it.

BD

I had money coming in from different sources and I kept putting some away in a special church account in the bank. When we were getting ready to build the church and people asked, "Where are we going to get the money?"

"Well," I said, "I know a fellow who's got twelve thousand dollars that he'll let you have."

"Oh, who's that?"

I said, "It's me; I've been saving it all along."

So we started off with that.

Merle Wagner was a great church worker as well, and he said, "If you build the church, then I'll build the parsonage. They have to have a place for the minister." I'd already built a little house on Lady Hammond Road for the minister but it was very small and wouldn't do as a parsonage. So Merle built the parsonage, and we set in to build the church.

Harry Renfree had some pictures of a church we liked, and we worked off those. That was all we had. I drew up sketches and framing plans and so on, and that's what we made it with.

Harry Renfree

BD had a group of volunteers working on the concrete foundation for the schoolroom basement, and I had a rather laughable experience soon after arriving. I came over to where they were working, and it was getting quite dark. Trying to be helpful, I picked up a barrel of wet concrete, took it over to where they were dumping it, and dumped my load. I couldn't see the person below because it was too dark, but I called out to him, "How was that?"

His only reply was "That will do for now." I learned later that I had dumped a good part of the load over him, but he never brought it up.

BD

I'd have perhaps six or eight fellows come but nobody to lead them. I'd go as their foreman and show them what to do and lay out the work for them. A couple of them were postmen, another fellow was a shoemaker; didn't have one carpenter amongst the whole bunch. They'd come after work and stay till dark.

We didn't know what a power tool was back then. All the truss work and everything was cut by hand. We generally had a good sharpener. If you had a poor sharpener, you didn't get along very well. I used to go down to the docks and pick up stuff. They had packing crates in those days and a fellow would save stuff for us. I got a whole bay for forty dollars: western pine, lovely stuff but all short pieces. I thought we could use it to make trusses for the church and got a fellow to deliver it. We got some long timber to go with it and laminated the trusses right there on the ground. We built them with legs and stood down at the bottom and put an anchor in and hoisted them up with ropes one after the other, like raising a barn.

I put some of my own men on the job at my expense to try to shove it on some so we could get clear of the bad weather and work inside. Hartford Horne did the shingling. The funny thing was that thirty-three years later the same man shingled the roof for the second time. He was working on his own then and had his boys with him.

Most of the fellows couldn't get off during the day and I'd get the stock we needed for the night. We strung lights and they would stay working till eleven at night. They'd work half as hard again as they would during the day. I remember one night we were stringing lights pretty well up in the peak. Arthur Layton went up the ladder, and Ches Pye offered to hold it. Ches wasn't very handy with anything, but he was always willing to help and do everything he could. We had to get way up and Ches balanced the ladder until Arthur, who was heavier than Ches, got too far out. Over it went and Arthur went down behind the seats. We took him to the hospital and when we came back, we heard a funny noise behind the seats. There was Ches just waking up. He had been knocked out cold and we never saw him at all.

Ches Pye used to go around preaching quite a bit. The deacon of one church told me that Mr. Pye was a wonderful man but when he got talking and ran out of the truth, he just kept going. He used to exaggerate quite a bit.

Old Milton Hubley used to come over after working at his ready-mix plant and he was a handy old fellow. He laid all the floor tiles—didn't want any help. He was very particular and did them all himself. He must have been sixty-five then.

The church didn't hire anybody; it was all volunteer work. We started in the fall and opened the church the next April.

Reg Short

My wife and I were married at Mulgrave Park Church. BD had quite an influence on our lives, as he did on a lot of other people's. We went on a campaign after the church was built and BD wanted some of the men to take part. He talked about giving; was a strong believer in tithing. I started looking at myself and realized that I wasn't doing very much and there was a lot more one could do. BD said, "You'll never have anything unless you give it away." It is so true, and it has worked out that way for us to this day. We never gave a penny or a dollar that we had to stop and wonder about. We never missed it. I think the more you put money as your priority the less you seem to have. He taught us just the reverse: not to worry about holding on to it. At Mulgrave Park Church, apart from just building the church, he influenced an awful lot of men in this business of tithing. The giving in that church has been a model for the Convention which goes on to this day, and it was due basically to his leadership.

Chapter 6
Helping out

*I got on as well, maybe better, than some
of those who wouldn't do anything to
help out.*

Laurie Stevens

He knew what it was like to be a nobody. When he worked for
his grandmother and at the furniture factory, he was a nobody,
and he knew what it was like to be at the bottom of the barrel.
But he knew what he was capable of, so it was easy for him to
relate to other people who thought they were nobody. He could
accomplish things, and he just expected that anybody else of his
ilk could accomplish things too. He always trusted them to do
something or at least to try.

I don't know how many subcontractors Dad developed. Year
after year there'd be new subcontractors who he'd encouraged
to go on their own. I don't know how many there were:
electricians, heating and plumbing contractors—he'd con-
tinually set them up and they'd develop into reasonably good
businessmen. A number of them wanted him to participate in
their companies. "Oh no, no, that's yours. You make it go." He
could have owned fifty percent of all of them, with no extra effort

or finances or anything else. But that wasn't his way. His way was to let them be self-sufficient.

Andrew Levy

I had been working with the heating contractor for some time, and one day we had a little dispute, and he told me I could go about my business, and that was it. I said, "Fine, sir, and thank you." The next day, Saturday, I went to see a friend and told him what had happened. He called BD and told him there was a fellow here maybe looking for work. BD asked who it was. "Andrew."

"Well, send him right over." When I got there, he jumped up and said, "I was hoping you would do this and start to work for yourself. Anything I can do to help, let me know. Can you do our work? .... Fine, you've got our work."

So I left there, and that Tuesday I ordered ten furnaces. They said, "You haven't any credit, Andrew. You'll have to do something about that." I never had five cents to my name. So I went over to see Mr. Stevens and told him what was wrong. "No problem, Andrew," he said. "Doris type up some letters guaranteeing Andrew's credit so he can give them to his suppliers." One day later I went into a manager's office, and he said, "Boy, those Stevens people must think a lot of you."

"Why?"

"Well, there's no limit on your credit here; you can have anything you want."

When people would ask how I got into business so quick with no money to start, I used to tell them I had a million dollar's credit.

One day BD came to me and said, "Andrew, you should have a house of your own." He believed a man should have his own house.

"Oh, my dear man, I can't afford a house. I have no money."

"Oh, you don't need money; I can arrange it."

Well, I borrowed $1,000 from my father, then BD got a mortgage for me from Canada Permanent for $2,000 and he put up the other $2,000 and that's how I got my first home. Whenever I think of my prosperity, I think of BD. He helped all of us, and I imagine that he probably helped half the guys who worked for him to get their own homes.

I remember when Russell Spence got out of jail, BD was there to meet him. He said, "It's time you straightened up." And he set him on his feet. Russell did all the foundations along Rowe Avenue.

Laurie Stevens

Dad had a favourite expression from Luke, "Those to whom much is given, much is expected." He used to say it a lot, and he believed it. One time he was talking to Russell Spence who had been in Dorchester and who Dad had helped to get going again. Russell had had a good year and after talking a while about how his business was going, Dad said to him, "Those to whom much is given, much is expected."

"BD," Russell said. "What does that mean?"

"It means, if you don't give, you don't get."

Andrew Levy

Ambrose Crow was another. He was often blind drunk but he still had a job, and in the end BD had him going to church with him. If there was a way of helping a man he would go to the full extent. He would never give up.

BD

It was not common then to help other tradesmen get started. But I got on as well, maybe better, than some of those who wouldn't do anything to help out.

Wayne Langley

Work was organized and work was steady, and he went way out of his way to keep men employed. He did it both as a matter of principle and as a matter of business. It was a year-round affair with his people. And he was always trying to teach people, whether senior carpenter or junior people. If he saw what you were doing and had a suggestion he would always take time to make that suggestion ... either, here's an easier way, or a better way, or have you thought of—people would react to that. He knew everyone's job and could do it. That's the way he would build a team. I would say that now that I've been in business myself, he practiced an awful lot of modern management techniques. Showing by example, trying to teach and develop, but not put down, building good bonds with his people, encouraging them to go on, to improve. I'm talking 40 years ago. So you might say he was old-fashioned and simple, but on the other hand, if he was managing a business today, he would be considered very current.

Laurie Stevens

Dad used to go down on Saturday night and bail a guy who worked for him out of jail. He'd bring him home, give his wife some money, and say, "Now don't give him any of that. Sober him up and get him to work on Monday morning." He was a tremendous worker, but give him his pay on Friday night and he was gone.

At Christmas time, we (L.B. Stevens Ltd.) give a certificate for a turkey, but with Dad, it had to be the actual physical bird. Because if you gave a guy a cheque or a certificate he might go spend it on booze. Ever since I was a kid, I've had to deliver those stupid birds. And then we made up bags of oranges and peanuts. He'd say, "You'd better take something more to the so and so's because his wife just won't get any more money out of him." We had to give something extra to the family regardless of what he thought of the guy. And animal candy—I don't know if you remember animal candy, but he was the world's worst for buying animal candy. It was almost unfair sometimes: the regular guys got a turkey, the guys who weren't so good got extra plus maybe a twenty-dollar bill to get some groceries for the family for Christmas Day.

BD

Some fellows were putting in the overpass to Fairview and they had two or three men trying to blast the bank away. They had been putting in pot holes and blasting but were getting nowheres. They came to me and asked if I knew a good dynamite fellow. I said, "I know a good man if you can keep him sober; Ruben Fleet. The main thing is don't give him any money on the weekend; pay him the first of the week, because if you pay him on the weekend, he won't be back until the middle of the next week."

Ruben got them to drill deep holes from the top, and also two down below. They drilled for a week or more and didn't blast a thing. That worried them, and they asked me if he was ever going to get done. I told them to leave him alone another week. Well, he pretty near blew the whole bank off in one shot. She just rolled out, the whole thing. They said they guessed the old fellow knew what he was doing. He had worked with me a lot.

I heard later that he was in bad shape. He drank every cent he earned, so he had nothing to live on. He was just living around anywhere. I went and found him and took him to our nursing home. He used to stand around in the wet, drilling, and when they pulled his boots off, it pretty near turned you sick just to look at his feet. He died there at the home. He was a good man, other than his drinking, a good old fellow.

Wayne Langley

There was one guy, a British guy and an ex-merchant marine, who had survived being torpedoed twice during the war. He put in BD's basements and foundations. This guy was as tough as anything and he'd start the day around seven-thirty by chewing tobacco, then he'd have a cigarette, then a pipe, then he'd chew tobacco again—all through the day. He was not a church man at all. But he was a hard worker, a hard drinker, though never on the job, a hard smoker—a hard everything. He was one of the people BD kept year-round. He never had much to say for BD, or anyone, except one time when I was saying that something we were doing was old fashioned. He said to me. "You may be right, and I don't know what you're learning at university," (he'd never got past grade two) "but I know he's helped me a lot. If it wasn't for BD, I'd be in the hospital, or an alcoholic. I wouldn't be working. Don't take what you're learning in school as everything. He knows what he's talking about."

Reg Short

Thirty years ago on New Year's Day we went in to see BD about getting a house. He said, "Come on, let's get in the car and I'll show you all our property." He discouraged us from coming to Dartmouth and wanted us to stay in the Mulgrave Park area, but we went over to see Laurie who was starting these houses in the Woodlawn area. Laurie was living in an old farm house where the Woodlawn Mall is now. He had a Volkswagen car and he had to drive through a cow pasture to this house which was roof tight and had a furnace in it, but the basement floor had not been finished. They had about twenty other houses started and in various stages on the street. It was nothing but mud. We chose this particular house and thought it would do as a start. We're still here thirty years later.

We didn't really have enough money to buy a house at the time. In those days you needed a $3,500 down payment on a house like ours, which cost $15,800. Laurie said he'd take $500 off because we were buying it directly through him and he gave us three years' insurance.

But the problem was that we only had $2,000, which was quite a lot for a young couple. We went to the bank and the bank manager wouldn't lend it to us because my salary wasn't able to handle it. BD said, "Have faith, it will all work itself out, just go ahead and move in. It's your house."

So we moved in on the twenty-fourth of May and then we had to figure out where to get the extra $1,500. And things did work out because two of his men were looking for a place to board. They noticed we didn't have any children, and they knew we had three bedrooms. I came back and asked Betty if she would take in boarders.

Betty Short

Me, take in a boarder? Me, prepare meals? I wasn't that good at getting meals in those days—not that I'm that good now—but anyway, we always were adventuresome. So the men came and stayed with us for about a year, and the fun part was that I did learn to cook. They put the food on our table, and we were able to go back to the bank and get the loan. And within the year we had the loan all paid off. It's an example of faith, and BD was good that way. He helped an awful lot of young people get started in business and to establish homes.

Reg Short

Nowadays all these new subdivisions are being built for people who want something bigger and fancier and don't really need it. There are none being built for people like we were thirty years ago. He built for the ordinary man, and I would say that we need a BD today.

Betty Short

Mrs. Stevens was quiet and gracious and kept in the background, but she was a very strong person. I'd say she was a stabilizing factor. She didn't get ruffled easily even though she never knew when BD was going to walk in with someone for a meal. You've heard of the pot of soup on the stove that you can just keep adding water to. Well, that was no joke. BD used to say that if they all wanted to come, they'd just put the soup in the bathtub and keep adding water. I have just lovely memories of her.

I'll always remember sitting talking to Laurie and his mother after he had graduated from Acadia and TUNS. That was when Laurie said he would come into the family business with his Dad. I can just see her beaming now; she was so happy.

Laurie Stevens

I started working with Dad in 1957. I went with him when he went blind. He had to have operations for cataracts. In those days it used to take a year or so between operations. You'd operate on one and then have to wait for the other one. So from '57 to '59 he was sort of laid up and I went to work for him for two years. I told him I would come for two years and then leave.

53

The year I started with him I was running around getting my feet wet. I didn't know everything that was going on. A girl who worked for him, Doris Baker, did his filing. One time I was looking in the safe for some bonds for the Department of Highways and couldn't find them. Doris said, "Oh, just a minute," and she ran to the filing cabinet and pulled them out. There was nine thousand dollars worth of bonds in the filing cabinet—which is like one hundred thousand today–and they were bearer bonds. Anybody could have picked them up and cashed them. I said, "Doris who told you to put them there?"

"Your father."

"And they were filed under bonds ?"

"Well, what else would you put them under ?"

"Why didn't you put them in that little safe?"

"He told me to put them in the file so he'd know where they were."

At the end of two years I told him I was leaving. "Well," he said, "I think you should look at staying in the business." I told him I didn't want anything to do with it. He talked quite a bit and said he thought I should go and see Gordon Cowan, the lawyer. Gordon told me, "Your father thinks you should set up your own company, separate from him. It would have nothing to do with your sisters. He thinks that's your biggest fear—that if you take over his business you're going to owe them something." I had six sisters which meant I had six brothers-in-law. "We have a scheme where all the buildings your dad owns will be sold to a trust which will go to your sisters." So I set up L.B. Stevens Construction.

About the time I was starting out, I was having a rough time getting money. I could only borrow five thousand from the bank, and that wouldn't build many houses. The local sales manager from a drywall manufacturer wanted us to use drywall. At first I told him I was using plaster, but then I thought drywall wasn't so bad. To make a long story short, I went to him a while later and offered to use drywall if they would sell me two carloads a week from May to November and give me ninety days to pay for it. He said, "We can't do that."

"Well it's just an offer. Think about it."

He came back in two or three weeks and agreed, on the condition we would use it in all our houses. He was looking at Dad and my uncle's business as well, of course. I wasn't going to use two carloads a week. Maybe three carloads for the summer would have done it for me.

I went to two other guys in the building trade and sold each of them a carload a week. I was paying $36.50 which was the wholesale price, and I offered them a carload a week for $35.50 but they had to pay me in thirty days. I also bought half my materials for twenty-five houses from both of them. One of them took me away to a housebuilder's convention in January of the next year and finally got round to asking me how much I was paying for drywall. I told him $36.50. "Well," he said, "you're selling it to us for $35.50. You're losing money."

"No, I'm not," I said. "I'm getting two carloads a week. You're paying me in thirty days and I've got ninety with them. That gives me eight weeks. How much money is that."

"Well that's about thirty-five or forty thousand dollars."

"That's my cash flow. That's how I'm building these houses. The dollar I'm losing is worth about 8% interest and that's all I'm paying."

"Son of a gun," he said. "I was worried you were buying it cheaper than we were."

That's how I got my first financing. I had a five thousand-dollar line of credit at the bank and the forty thousand I was rolling with the drywall people. As long as I didn't end up with more than five houses at Christmas time, we didn't owe anybody any money. My father didn't even know about it. I didn't sell any to him.

My mother was always serene. Dad would get enthused about things and do them quickly. She would say, "Burnett, are you sure you're doing right?" "Yep," he'd say. She was always the moderator. I had a little business before I went to Acadia. I had a concrete mixer and a truck. Both he and Mom wanted me to go to university. Then he turned around and sold the truck and the mixers to Cyril Hubley, who later owned Dartmouth Readymix.

I had gone away, but usually in the winter you didn't pour concrete anyway, not in those days. When I came home in the spring I asked where the mixers were. "Oh they're around." He was very evasive.

"Where's the truck?"

"Well, I sold it."

"You sold my truck ?"

I was so mad, I just was livid.

After that I wouldn't speak to him for a while. My mom said to me, "You're making a mistake. You shouldn't get mad at him." She always supported him. When I think back now it meant a lot. It didn't then. I was seventeen and so mad I was beside myself. She always tried to encourage everyone to come around to his side. It was amazing how she'd support him.

Dad had helped lots of people get started and I guess he helped me, too, but in this case he did it through a lawyer. My wife and I stayed here instead of going to Vancouver. I set up L.B. Stevens Construction and he had B.D. Stevens, and we ran both of them side by side and still do. Twenty-five years later I bought the ready-mix company from Cyril Hubley, and we also bought some of Dad's other companies, like the nursing home.

Chapter 7
A Turning Point

Did you ever build a church?

Laurie Stevens

One time while I was going to Acadia, and Dad was partly blind, I drove him and Abner Langley to Moncton to hear a man called LaTourneau speak. He gave us his book, *Mover of Men and Mountains*. A very dynamic guy, almost overbearing, really—a very strong-willed person. But the story he had to tell was just fantastic.

BD

I remember they brought LaTourneau a plate of food and he said, "Take that aside, I can eat any time. I've come to talk to people. I'll just tell them some of my experiences and what the Lord has done for me over my life." He told great stories. He told how when he was building tractors and dozers, he had a whole bunch to sell. They had about a dozen agents out selling, and they couldn't get rid of them. He said he was going to sell some himself, so he went down the road and found a fellow digging a cellar with a pair of horses and a scoop. He asked, "Could you use a dozer."

"I certainly could, but I can't afford one."

"I'll have one sent to you, and when you get the money you can pay me." So he did. It wasn't long before the man bought it and went into business. He bought about a dozen more through the years. LaTourneau said he had faith in the man and it was worth it to give him a machine to get started. I understood that.

He said he had a prayer meeting in his shop every morning at nine o'clock. He had about three hundred people working for him, and they all had to come to the prayer meeting. First of all, he had held it early in the morning, but some wouldn't get there, so he knocked off fifteen minutes in the middle of the day, right when everything was rushed. He said he had ended up paying for their prayer meeting.

I never heard tell of LaTourneau before he came to Moncton. He flew to the meeting in his own plane, spoke to us and flew back home to Texas. He was a wonderful man. I had his book but I lent it so often I don't have it anymore.

When he got through explaining all his experiences—his favourite one four times—he came around to the tables, and he put his hand on my shoulder and said, "Now, son, what do you do for a living?"

"I'm in the contracting business. I build houses and other buildings sometimes."

"Did you ever build churches?"

"I helped to build two."

"You should be building churches. You have to have somebody building churches here in the world. I know the building is not the Church, but they have to have buildings to worship in. Now, when you get home from here, before long there will be a couple of fellows coming to see you wanting you to build a church."

For a few days I didn't pay much attention to my work or anything. I was just getting ready to see what would happen. I felt it would be something real. Sure enough, one morning two men came into my office and said, "We heard you might be interested in building a church for us."

I said, "I don't know about that." It ended up that I built the Shubenacadie United Church. It was one of the first ones I built after that meeting and there were over thirty more.

Before I really got going on building churches here I was going to go out to India. I even had my visa set up and everything. I got quite enthused about it. I had money set aside, about five thousand dollars which is more like thirty thousand today, and was to go out for 6 months with a missionary to help them to learn to build. But I took a heart attack about the time I was ready to go. I was in the hospital for six weeks—pretty near went for it that time. I had some good men on and they just carried on. The doctors said I would never be able to work again but I did more afterwards than before. I'm just as glad now I didn't go.

There were over two hundred men at that meeting in Moncton and I was the only one who went out and started to do things. There have been different things like that that have happened in my life. It was the inspiration I got at that meeting that started me going in earnest.

Rhodes Cooper

I remember very clearly the first meeting to talk about building that BD came to at St. Philip's Anglican Church. We were amazed that he was willing to join our team without looking for any return for himself at all. He just wanted to get busy and help us get our church built. My contact with people of other churches was limited, and I had been very wary of Baptists, but he sure dissipated that quickly. It was just his manner—his gentleness and his openness. I had just arrived there as the new rector. They had a little converted army hut as a mission hall, and we had financial problems, but we got going.

When we were building the church we were able to get a crane from the dockyard to raise the trusses, which we had built on the floor. There were wind warnings but we thought we would proceed. At the end of the day we had six or eight secured. My sister was living with us at the time, and she came home about eleven o'clock. The wind was very high, and she said she had gone by the church but had not noticed the trusses. That got me worried. So I went up and looked. I just wept, I wept buckets. Those trusses were down, some of them smashed through the floor into the basement. It was just destruction. I wept the night over it. It was a very, very sad night that night.

That Sunday I cast aside the sermon I had planned and preached on Job and how he came had come out of his affliction. A week later every one of those trusses was rebuilt and ready to go up again. The response of the community was absolutely fantastic. People we had never seen before turned up to do volunteer labour. In a way the destruction made us pull up our socks.

Wayne Langley

I worked on three churches in Halifax. One was St. Philip's at Bayers Road and Connaught when the hurricane came along. We had the floor down; it was a particularly strong floor of two-by-fours on edge, all spiked together. The beams were up for the wall and we had major rafters up for the roof. We knew the storm was coming and secured it as best we could. But the storm drove some of those rafters right straight through the floor. It was unbelievable. We went back and tore all the superstructure down again. It took days to repair the floor because you had to pry all those two-by-fours apart to get out the broken ones, and lay in the new ones.

BD

It was no more than a week before the accident that I had gone and put insurance on the St. Philip's work. We normally did it with all our work, and it seemed right. It was a good thing I did. We cut all the trusses up for firewood and started again. It was a bit of a struggle with the insurance company, but we didn't lose a cent. Funny how things turn out.

Rhodes Cooper

I was also really jolted the night of that first meeting for St. Philip's and I remember it very clearly because BD said, "Until I have given my tithe I don't really believe I have started to give. I only begin to give after I get over that ten percent." Well, that shook a lot of people, and I went home and talked to my wife about it, and that was the beginning of tithing in our household. We give our tithe to the church, and then anything else that comes along, we give to fairly generously as well.

I left St. Philip's twenty-three years ago and have been to Newfoundland and New Brunswick, and now I'm back in Nova Scotia. We do not talk much about tithing in the Anglican Church, but it is beginning to spread. Last September our senate had a stewardship meeting, and oh, it was so pessimistic I couldn't take it any longer. I got up and bore witness to the tithing my wife and I had done through the years. First of all a clergyman got up and said, "I don't know if Ken Cooper knows this, but my wife and I are tithers because of a similar speech he gave some years ago." There must have been four or five people at that meeting who then said the same kind of thing.

BD helped us at St. Philip's but his influence went much further than that one congregation. Our whole financial picture has changed here in Bedford since I've come. Our giving has more than doubled, primarily because I'm a convinced tither, and I've preached, taught and encouraged it. It was BD who got me going, and I still live by his example.

Chapter 8
Churches for New Communities

We can't just always have people we like.
We need to learn to like those that's hard
to like, and love those that's hard to love.

BD

It was through the laymen's groups that I built a lot of the churches. One on P.E.I started that way. And one would lead to another. It was mostly through travelling and working with laymen's groups that I came to build churches.

Harry Renfree

I travelled a lot with him, visiting various laymen's groups and the like. One time a number of us were travelling to Moncton for a stewardship meeting. There was about a half a dozen of us in BD's car. One was a lady who really didn't have a greatly developed sense of humour. After a while, BD told a story of a drunk who came back late at night to a housing estate where the houses were very much alike. He went up to one house and tried the key and it didn't work, so he went up to a second house and it didn't work there either. He was making quite a row. Finally a lady poked her head out of the window and shouted down to him, "Look here my man, you've got your key in the wrong lock." His reply was, "Oh be quiet, you old goat, you've got your head out the wrong window." A few miles down the road the good lady turned to BD and said, "Mr. Stevens, did he get in? That's what I want to know?"

We also had with us an Irish evangelist, who was himself quite a humorist. On the way back he was telling a lot of Irish stories and this same lady asked BD, "Do you think the stories that man is telling are true?" BD's laughing answer was, "I don't think so, Miss, but we'll have to humour him; he's a visitor." We stopped at Amherst for a coffee. It was at the Terminal Lunch, and BD asked the waitress if it had anything to do with the Last Supper.

Another time I was eating in a restaurant with BD and he ordered a steak. It came out very rare and he told the waitress, "I've seen cattle on the hoof wounded as badly as that and live."

Reg Short

When he went to buy a new car he went in dressed very casually as usual, and the salesmen who were experienced payed no attention to him. He asked one what they wanted for a Cadillac and they said, "You're not interested in that one." You know how it goes. So BD walked out, I guess, and went to the other dealer and bought the car, and then drove back to the first dealer and showed them the car. He told them, "Never judge a man by what he wears." I guess that's what he said.

Harry Renfree

I remember that Cadillac, the only one he ever owned, and he didn't care too much for that. Soon after he had it, he drove up one time and opened the back door and out fell some shovels and picks and so on, which looked a bit strange in a Cadillac. He was a man of no pretentions and was always the way you found him.

He hardly fit the Cadillac image because he was a man of simple tastes but he liked big cars.

One time BD wanted to get down below Chester to see Will Heisler, one of our members who hadn't been well. It was midwinter, early February, and a dirty day. The two of us started out. The snow was heavy and the road hadn't been plowed. Finally we came head on to the snowplow coming the other way. BD managed to get off to the side. He rolled down the window and looked up at the man and said, "You needn't bother going any farther; I've plowed it all the way from Halifax."

On another occasion BD must have been moving a little too quickly, or he went quickly past a stop sign or something like that, because a motorist pulled alongside him and said he should wait because a policeman wanted to speak to him. At the time Halifax had some mounted policemen on traffic patrol. After a while, the policeman came up on a horse and proceeded to give BD a ticket. His response was, "Well, if you're going to catch me again you'd better get a better rig than that."

He was a big man, a man of few words, very quiet, serene almost, but he always had a bit of humour for the occasion.

BD

I remember going down to a church behind Kentville, back over the mountain. The minister there was Sam Baxter, and he wanted me to organize a men's group. He said the men would bring their women to church and sit on the pole fence and tell yarns and chew tobacco while the service was going on, and then they'd take their wives home.

In those days I'd get the names of the men and send them a personal letter telling them I was coming, and then I'd go down and spend a day going about talking with them. You've got to get down next to them, working in the fields and the like. One thing that got them started that time was that they formed a men's choir. They liked to sing. They never knew a note or anything, just sang. They even got a new organ for the church, they liked it so well. It made a big difference to that church. Before, they'd had a hard time paying their minister, but once the men started singing and going to church they always had enough money.

I told a lot of men they should get up and read scripture and lead in prayer. They had never done this, you see. One fellow was in politics and was a great talker, and I got him to read scripture. He fumbled so and after a while he said, "I guess that's all I can read this morning." Yet he could talk politics by the hour. I remember another man who was to lead the prayers asked if he could write it down. He said he had never said a prayer in his life. I said, "If you like, as long as you say what you mean. The Lord is listening to you, not us fellows."

I could often do better than a minister because I talked the men's language. And I wasn't afraid to say what I thought. It's funny how one man talks to another; it's different than when a minister tries to do it. I found it very easy to talk face to face.

I remember going to New Ross when they were putting on a drive to raise money. At one man's house I visited there were two International trucks sitting in the yard that had never been used. He said he always gave twenty-five dollars a year to the church. I said, "I'd be ashamed to give that. I see you have two trucks worth $50,000 each and you don't even need them. Here you are buying trucks with the Lord's money instead of giving it to the church."

"Well, I'll go up to one hundred dollars, but no more."

"That's all right—that's between you and the Lord."

"I heard you were a hard man to deal with," he said, "and I guess you are."

Most of my expenses those days were travel. I had a new white Buick, and I put ninety-two thousand miles on it in two years.

Andrew Levy

I remember we went to Bridgewater once in a new Buick to help start a laymen's group there. On the way we picked up old Mr. Hubley who was a concrete man and who had done a lot of work with BD. We went to a restaurant for dinner and Mr. Hubley ordered lobster while the rest of us just had an ordinary dinner.

BD whispered to the waitress about paying for the group, and old Mr. Hubley was so upset, I don't think he enjoyed his dinner much because he had figured on paying for himself. Nope, BD payed the works and wouldn't even take a cent from anyone for gas.

He always seemed to have money, always seemed to be blessed; he never seemed to wonder or worry. If a boys' group needed some money or someone was in trouble he'd say, "I'll whip you a few bucks on the side." Sometimes he'd call me over and say, "I've got a hundred to give towards this or fifty dollars towards that." I don't know how many times he gave me money just to help out without ever saying a thing about it—no credit on income tax or anything. He just gave it.

Coming back from Bridgewater that night, I was driving and he said, "Step her up a bit, Andrew." We had an airforce fellow with us, and when we got to about one hundred and twenty miles an hour, I slacked her off a bit. "Why'd you slack her off Andrew," he asked. "A few more miles and we'd have been airborn."

BD

At the Baptist Convention one year, they asked me if I would go on a drive to raise money for the "Churches for New Communities" drive. I said that I wasn't such a good talker but I would go if they could get someone to talk for me. So Abner Langley decided to go with me. It took a lot of planning to get ready. Abner was a great organizer, and we took pamphlets and literature with us to the churches.

Often they weren't too sympathetic towards us. It was the first time it was ever done here—the only time. We were gone from home for most of six months.

A farmer who had a team of oxen was crossing a railway track with a companion when they heard a train coming. The farmer started to beat one of the oxen to get across the tracks quickly. Later the companion asked him why he'd only beat the one oxen, and the farmer said that the other one never did anything anyway; it just went along, so what was the use of beating it. So I mostly went after the busy people wherever we were.

One time Abner and I were down near Digby and couldn't get anyone to help. I went to see a fellow who was a politician. He was also in the insurance business, and he was awful busy. I said, "You're so interested in looking after yourself, you don't have time for others and the Lord's work."

"I go to church."

"I didn't say you didn't go to church; going to church doesn't make you a Christian. I said you don't have time to work for others. You just work for yourself."

"I am very busy."

"If you're busy you can always find time. That's why I came to see you," I said.

He said he wasn't very good at talking to people. I said, "Look, at election time you can get up there and talk about things that are never even going to happen." Well, we talked until pretty near four o'clock in the morning. He ended up doing a great job for us, going around organizing people in various churches to go on committees to raise money for new churches.

One time we drove through from Yarmouth to Moncton where we had arranged a meeting and Abner took laryngitis and could hardly talk. So he said I would have to speak at the meeting. We went in and the church was full. I got up and said, "When I took on this job it was to drive the fellow around who was going to do the talking, and there he is sitting down there, and he can't say a thing. Now I'll tell you the best I can what we are trying to do, and I want you people to help us." I explained to them that it wasn't churches, only people, that was what we were striving for. I told them that the building is not the Church, the building is where the people meet, and it is the people who are the Church. But we needed buildings.

If you just talk along in an ordinary way you don't have to make a speech. When I got through, the whole church pledged. It was the biggest pledge we'd ever had. Abner said, "I guess I'll do the driving from now on and you can do the talking."

For six months we went all over the Maritimes raising money. We got all the churches to give each Sunday in a special envelope that was sent to the head office in Wolfville. That's the way the money came in. Then head office would lend money to new churches interest-free for the first three years. The fund is still going, and it has over four million dollars into it now. It has helped a lot of churches.

The year I was president of the Convention I visited two to three hundred churches. They were mostly small churches, and some of them had never seen a Convention president. The big churches always had lots of visits, but I decided when I became president that I would visit the smaller ones.

Many of the little churches had never thought of having a layman's group for example. When I visited them as president, I spoke mostly about the value of holding together, explaining that if we stand together we are much stronger than if we are separate.

We can't just always have people we like; we need to learn to like those that's hard to like, and love those that's hard to love. We were meant to stand together, and Christian fellowship holds us together. Generally I'd also take their morning service. That way I'd get to know them better.

I was anxious that people understood what the Convention stood for and how much value it had for us. I didn't go to preach to them; I went to explain that if we stood together, we could do much more in our work. It gives you a big lift to go into these churches and change things, even just a little bit.

People often invited me to stay in their homes. I seldom went to hotels. I liked to stay in people's homes; gave me a chance to have a real talk with people and get far better acquainted. That way too they'd noise it around that I was coming to talk to the group. Just to speak in a church doesn't get you anywheres much. You get a lot more done by talking to people in their homes.

Laurie Stevens

He thought the world of the people who worked for him, and of course they thought the world of him. The year he was president

CHURCHES FOR NEW COMMUNITIES

of the Baptist Convention, he had nobody in the office except one girl, Doris Baker, and the rest were all carpenters. He was building all kinds of things, and he'd say, "You guys look after it, I've got to go to New Brunswick, I've got to go here, or I've got to go there." And he did, he travelled all over the place, and yet somehow they managed.

BD

John MacKay was a chartered accountant who had retired and came to work with me part-time. The year I was president of Convention, he was sure my business was going to fail up. One morning he said, "This church work you're doing is all very well and good but if you keep on you're going to lose your business." He gave me quite a talking to.

I said, "When I took this job on, I promised the Lord that I would look after his work if he would look after mine."

"Oh, that's all right, but you should pay more attention to your own work."

"Well, I'm going to keep going, Let me know if I'm going to fail up so's I'll be home."

In the fall he told me there was something wrong. He said, "I can't see how it happened myself but this is the biggest year you've ever had."

Abner Langley

He was a man with vision; he saw how things would develop when others didn't. He saw where churches needed to be built because of population shifts and new communities. He saw how Bridgeview was going to be built up, and the opportunity. And he saw that the Convention needed to raise its whole level of giving. He was the only layman ever to be elected president.

I had been president two years before BD was elected president of the Convention. He came to me one afternoon and we spent a couple of hours talking about the budget and the need to raise the level of giving. He said we had to change our whole pattern. He lifted our sights to about two and a half million dollars. When I had been president we would raise about four hundred thousand. I thought, "For once he has gone too far. He is too ambitious." But he felt he could do it, and I agreed to stand behind him at the Convention. It was BD who put the power to it. He raised the whole level of giving and we reached his goal.

Chapter 9
Bill Oliver

You look back over these things and
you wonder how we did it.

Bill Oliver

We'd had our struggles at Cornwallis. I'd been there for about twenty-five years. We'd paid off our bills and we reached the point where we knew we should be doing something different, something more. It was time for renovations and building, and what we had in mind was going to take some money.

I can't recall the specific occasion when I first met BD, but it was during the war years, and it was particularly around the West End Baptist during the ministry of Abner Langley. Abner and I had been classmates, and he told me about the wonderful things that BD was doing for them. BD's work at West End became a model for all the churches in convocation. He woke everyone up. We had to go through more or less the same procedure that they had gone through at West End—real giving and real pledges and commitment.

I talked to BD and he seemed interested in helping us. I thought he would look after the technical aspects of building, and it would be up to me to raise the sights of the congregation, but I found I didn't even have to do that alone.

His reputation as a contractor didn't rest so much on how he worked with tools and buildings, it was the spirit in which he worked. It was not just a matter of doing the job, but he involved people in such a way that they'd be better people for having done the job. It turned out it was the same with his church work.

BD

When I first went there to Cornwallis Church it was falling down. They had no Sunday school facilities, and they were meeting down in the basement, in a little hole. And they were very poor givers. It was more like a social centre than a church.

Bill asked me to come and see what I could do. I went to a couple of meetings, and then Bill asked me to come and preach for one Sunday. I said, "All right, but I'm not going to preach the way you do. It will be more of a lecture." I thought the thing over a bit and decided, that before I was going to help them I wanted some understanding on the whole thing—whether they're going to play their part or whether they expected me to do it all. Bill said, "You tell them right out straight what's going on."

So I went and I said, "I'm not going to come here and help you if you continue to lead the life you are leading. I see you outside the tavern—even your deacons. You go around begging at a few stores to pay your minister and put a few cents in yourselves. What's the idea? This is the Lord's work, and I won't help you if you won't help yourselves. You should be paying your part." Bill told me afterwards that when I had started talking that way he thought they would get up and chuck me out. But they knew I was right. They were terrible for drinking.

Laurie Stevens

Nobody else would ever have gotten away with what he said to people in ordinary laymen's language. They would have been crucified for bigotry and everything else. But he would just come out and say it all, and it wouldn't bother him one little bit.

He was often almost domineering. He wasn't well enough educated not to be. What he saw as right was right, and if you didn't see it, then get out of his way. And yet he had a heart of gold. He would give anything to anybody. As long as he thought they were trying to do what was right, he would give them anything he had.

Bill Oliver

After we got things straightened away he would come to down to the prayer meetings and sit with the brotherhood, and with a little bit of humour and prayer and talk he would get people charged. He had this knack. The man gave people a sense of confidence, you see. You never felt that he was doing things to patronize people or for himself. You never felt that he was patting you on the head or anything like that. He was working along with you, and he was very quiet. But I always felt that when I approached BD I had to make sure I had done my homework. I never went half prepared. I used to tell my congregation, "Don't fool now. You've got to know what you want, and whatever I tell him that has to be it. He doesn't fool. There's a deep intellect there, and when he speaks, every word counts."

In terms of this world, he was a pretty influential man, but you wouldn't know it. He didn't throw his weight around; he moved around very humbly. The congregations of thirty or more churches he built will never know how much he assisted them, how much he got at a discount because of the respect and regard the merchants had for the man.

I think he was a very committed man. I think he was a grateful man. If he were to just let go and talk about himself sometime, he would tell you that God had been good to him. You see, he wanted to repay God. Because of that, he wanted to give everybody a chance.

If you measured up in any way at all, BD was going to give you a chance. He expressed his Christianity in a different way than some people do—it was not all just talk. His greatest witness was what he did and the way he did it; that was his message. I think in addition to what he said and the way he said it, there was the stance he took. It wasn't fanatical, but a firm, determined, steady, balanced, forward movement. It couldn't be stopped you see.

BD

We set up a pledge system and put a big board up on the wall with people's names on it and their pledges alongside so that everyone knew what the other fellow was giving and wouldn't be afraid to tell anybody else.

It turned out there were some good people amongst them, after they got on the right track. Every Sunday they marked their pledges on the board, even if it was only five dollars. If there was a fellow missing, they'd go to him and say, "Look, you missed your pledge this morning."

They had never raised money there before. But that time, we paid off forty thousand dollars, which is like a couple of hundred thousand now, in two years.

You look back over these things and you wonder how we did it.

Bill Oliver

In 1960 I became president of the Convention. BD had been president just before me. I don't know how many times his big cadillac would roll up to my door. I'd pack my bags and we'd go to New Brunswick or wherever. One time we were on the Island, and we went into a hotel to get a room. As it happened I was carrying the bags. BD asked for a room, and the clerk looked at him and then at me and then back at BD, and asked whether he wanted one room or two. BD said, "Yes, one is okay. He's never said anything before, so I guess he don't mind." Oh, he always had a little joke that went right to the point.

Pearleen Oliver

In the years of building up Cornwallis Street, I wasn't observing him much. All I knew was, here's a man of wealth—to us he was wealthy—and yet he's taking an interest. I mean we were in the slums of the city. I thought, well this is wonderful, it's God's doing, and I stayed out of the picture.

When Bill became president of Convention—the first black to become president—I was concerned about him. But I figured he was old enough to fight his own battles. BD seemed to know he might have some problems when he was travelling, and he always arranged to be a sort of guardian for him. These are just my impressions now, they might not be true. But I admired Mr. Stevens for taking time out of a busy professional life to assist Bill.

Bill Oliver

I don't think I really understood what was happening, to tell the truth, and I don't know whether I ever will. He helped me so much and seemed to anticipate what was going to happen. It was so unusual. BD was always there. He used to pick me up and off we'd go on a trip somewhere. The Convention never had too many men like him. I don't know whether they recognize it or not. The thing is, he never had to do what he did.

I never really thought about it then, but now, when I stop to think, someone was meeting all those travelling expenses. I guess it was BD and it makes me feel so ... moved ... so sad. I never thought.

Pearleen Oliver

It wasn't until when, darn it, we were going to build a new church at Beechville that I got to know him. That's the poorest community that you could ever find, and yet we said we were going to build a new church there. We couldn't stand worshipping in that old church that the slaves had built. People thought it was wonderful because the slaves had built it.

Now it was BD and I, because I was really the promoter of the new church. I'm not a bookkeeper by nature or education, but I had to keep account of every cent and where it went. I knew we needed every cent, and BD became my slave master, I guess you'd say. Even when he went to Florida, sometimes at eleven o'clock at night the phone would ring and it would be BD wanting to know the balance. I'd have to get out of bed and get all the reports out. I'd say, "It will take a while now and you're calling from Florida." He'd say, "That's all right, don't worry about the call."

I don't think he worked so well with women; I think his work was with men. I felt in the beginning he didn't count women on the same basis as men. That was maybe just me, but I felt it. And I was a black woman, too. At first it was just orders—well, not orders really, but you know. Then we got so we could carry on a conversation. But I knew I was being measured. And I said to myself, doggone it, I'm going to measure up. When he would ask, "What have we got there?" I had to have an answer. You had to be that way with him.

I felt at the end that he really had a great respect for me. And that's what I was aiming for, that he would know he could work with a woman, that she could be as capable as a man. For those three years I accounted for every cent, paid all the bills, and kept everything in order. Now I'm the type of person that's very forthright, and when I've got a job to do, I get geared up and I don't let much stand in my way. And I'm going to speak the truth. Well, it was a wonderful three years.

Just near the end I told him we wanted a big cross. We're not Catholics or anything, but we wanted a cross high up on that steeple. Some Baptists don't go in for that kind of thing. He said, "Why would you, a Baptist, want a cross up there?" He tried to explain that we mustn't put too much emphasis on the symbol of the cross and that there were deeper spiritual things. But he didn't give us too much hassle. When we drove in we—myself and the other women—we wanted to look up and see that cross.

The day they were putting the cross up, Mr. Stevens was there—the dear old soul, he was there before the men. They were using this great big crane, and they were putting it up the wrong way—it was just going to face the trees on both sides. We wanted to see the cross, not just the side of it, so I jumped out of the car and ran over to Mr. Stevens. I said, "Put it so it will face us when we drive into the churchyard, so we can see the cross."

He thought about it. The men were just standing there and the cross was hanging in the air. He went to the men and told them that Mrs. Oliver wanted the cross to turn the other way. Now these men knew how the cross should go; thought it should go as the architect had drawn it. Anyway, they turned that cross around. I could tell, some of them were a bit peeved. We had come at just the right time. If they had done it their way the cross would have been facing the woods where only the birds would see it.

I felt at first that BD was condescending, and that he was a man's man. I thought he felt he knew what was best for you and that he had a sort of missionary spirit. But when we were building that church, that church was in my heart and I came to see those feelings were more in me than him. He had so much goodness and sincerity. Mind you, he got to know us better too. I don't think, other than my husband, there is a man I respect more than BD.

BD

Bill Oliver came later to ask me if I could help get the men in the Beechville Housing Co-op organized. They had formed a co-op to build houses and they'd been at it a couple of years and couldn't get it going.

There were twelve men, and we started two houses. They were all supposed to work on the two until we got them pretty well along and then start two more. It was quite a little job to keep them all satisfied. They all wanted to build first. By the time we got it going it was getting cold, and they thought we couldn't start in the winter. I told them we built all winter. It was one of the hardest thing I ever had to get straightened out. It took me about three months to get it organized.

Laurie Stevens

There was one white fellow at Beechville. He had married a black girl and he was yapping at the meeting. Dad sat listening for a while and then he said, "You're the worst off coloured fellow here. Why don't you keep your mouth shut for a while. All the rest of these black fellows get along all right, you're the only problem here." Bill Oliver was just about devastated. Dad said to Bill, "This fellow is thinking up all kinds of things to say, and maybe it's just because he's white. Maybe we should paint him black and put him with the rest of them and then we'd get along just fine." Well after a while this fellow shut up, and they went ahead and built those houses. And they built him one too, and they got along fine. Somehow Dad got away with it.

Bill Oliver

The very fact is, they all knew he was the man who had developed Bridgeview. He was a big contractor, and he was out here with us. He led the prayer service Wednesday night and he spoke at the Sunday service. They had never had anyone work with them like that. That in itself gave them a sense of being somebody. We had three different groups studying co-op housing. Everybody else—government and everyone—were fighting and feuding over one another, and I told BD what I was trying to do. He'd be out there at seven in the morning; he'd sit there and get those fellows going. He had the patience, but he could be rough too. They knew he was there to help them.

BD

They had no money or credit, and I had to buy materials for them. I remember I sent out to the coast and got a carload of shingles for nine dollars a square. They are now about eighty dollars, so I saved them quite a lot of money one way and another. I had lots else going on at the time. I went there at nights, there was some cold nights out there, and Saturdays. I used to have to go rope them out of bed and get them going. I shoved the thing quite a little bit, and I could, because they knew I was giving a lot of my time. We started with twelve houses and ended up with thirty-six.

The brood when they lived in the garage in Fairview. Back, from left to right, Helen, Jean, Moana, in front, Laurie and Audrie.

The Maples, their second home in Halifax. It was demolished and apartments built on the site.

BD Stevens and Eva Redden at the time of their marriage.

"And it all came tumbling down." St. Philip's
Anglican Church before the wind struck.

Chapter 10
Newfoundland

"The Lord sent me to ask if you would go to Newfoundland." I said, "Are you sure it wasn't Abner Langley that sent you?"

BD

The Baptist Convention wanted me to go over to Newfoundland to see what I thought about building a church there. I told them that I didn't think we could ever start a church there; we couldn't find enough interested people to even start a church. That same year Dixon Burns, who was superintendent of the Missions for Western Canada, went over and set up a fellowship. Later he was talking to Abner Langley who's a great friend of mine. Dixon was looking for someone to spearhead the thing. He came to me and said, "The Lord sent me to ask if you would go to Newfoundland."

I said, "Are you sure it wasn't Abner Langley that sent you?"

He said, "To tell the truth it was."

I was reluctant about going. I was very busy, and I thought that to try to build a church with no people was pretty near impossible. But I went and we found a lot of American servicemen there, and they were for the biggest part Baptist, so they fell right into it. But we had quite a few ups and downs before we got started.

Freeman Fennerty

I was in Kentville when BD and Dr. Langley were involved in the "Churches for New Communities" drive. He came to see me then and later put the Newfoundland matter to me as a challenge. It really appealed to me. He said, "Come on over to Newfoundland as my guest." He didn't try to persuade me at all—he just said there was work there that needed to be done. If he hadn't come to see me I'd have stayed in Kentville.

BD had been going over for a while and wasn't impressed with the chances but they had formed a church and rented a room for meetings and had soon outgrown that. BD then built them a parsonage. They were using that and decided to build a building. They got plans drawn up and found they were way out of reach, and that's when BD really came into the picture. He said that if they let him build to his own plans, he'd build them a church for fifty thousand dollars, I think it was. No one knows how much it cost, but he said he'd do it for fifty thousand and he did. We went over, and he pointed out to me what had to be done to build the congregation. With my experience in church promotion work it really appealed—it was love at first sight. We went first to St. John's, and he was able to get the building details straightened out a couple of days early. It was in January and he said, "We have these days to spare, so let's go over to Corner Brook." So we went, and that was the beginning of that church. We were in Corner Brook a day and a half when a threatening snowstorm came up but we decided to go on to Stephenville anyway. We hired a taxi to take us. There was one place, Gallant's Hill, where the taxi got stuck, and BD and I pushed it up the rest of the hill. Oh, it was very blustery.

We were stuck in Stephenville for three days, so he said, "Let's go and make a few calls." And lo and behold, we came across three Baptist families, American servicemen, and that was the beginning of that. But the building of the churches at Stephenville and Corner Brook was more or less out on a limb for a time. At Corner Brook the Baptist Convention threw in fifty thousand dollars towards it, which was a big help. I was able to garner more financial resources to help out. With BD's expertise in building and getting donations of stuff we knew what to do. He didn't wait for everything to be guaranteed. If he felt it was possible, he didn't hesitate to jump in. That was the only trip we made together and I ended up over there for eight years.

BD

Otis Keddy was my foreman in Newfoundland. He had his troubles and often got discouraged, and he didn't want to stay. I'd get on a plane and go over and talk with him and get things straightened out. Every time we got straightened away, we'd have another upset.

Otis liked to fish, and there's fish in every little pond over there. As soon as he got through working, he wouldn't even bother to get his supper; he'd go fishing. I think that's the only thing that kept him there—he was so pleased to be able to fish.

We couldn't get help that would work. We got a couple of fellows off the boats who had never worked inland before, but they wanted to try it. I remember after the first weekend I paid them they didn't show up Monday morning. After a while, one fellow came staggering up, he'd been drunk. He said, "Skipper, I'm sorry but I met a lot of friends I hadn't seen for quite a while and they all treated me, and I'm in bad shape. Me buddy is down there laying in the gutter. He's worse than I am. I suppose you'll fire us."

I said, "Well, I don't know. If you sober up and stay with us, maybe not." Well, they both did, and they stayed with us and were great workers.

They weren't handy at all at this kind of work, but they'd try anything. They'd never used a pick and shovel before in their lives. We had to pick a trench for the footings and I went and got a couple of picks that were as big as anchors. After a while I saw one of them standing there hanging on to his hands. He said, "Skipper, you sure this is the right kind of instrument you've got us here?" He had been holding it way over his head and swinging it down to the ground. His hand was just stinging. I showed him how to pick, to just keep picking along. He said, "You'd better go over and show me buddy; he's pretty near killing himself, too. He don't know how to work this thing." They were pretty comical. They worked with us clear through to the end.

I didn't worry much about a fellow's trade, I just took any man who was willing to work, and in no time he either worked or he got out altogether. I always watched to see that they were good honest people who were willing to work. Even if they had their faults, you could overlook them if they were willing and anxious to keep going. I've found there is always a good streak in a person if you look for it.

When we were ready to send the stock over, we chartered a little boat and loaded everything on to it and sent it over from Halifax. It was February so there was a lot of ice when they left, and I thought that was the end of my cargo, that they'd get stuck in the ice. But all at once, one day, I got a call from a fellow who said, "Skipper, I want to know what to do with this stuff I got for you." It just happened that there was a plane going in about fifteen minutes, so I got right on it.

Andrew Levy

We flew in some old planes in those days—old bombers really—and they used to rattle like a bus. BD once said about flying, "I just close my eyes and say a prayer once she lifts off, and by the time I'm finished she's levelled off, that's all there is to it; never bothers me at all."

BD

I got there about four hours after I was talking to him on the phone. Here they were, unloading the bricks, and they were just dumping them. The bricks were all face brick, and you had to be careful with them. Oh, it was a near thing. I had windows and lumber and everything onto that little boat.

At the time I was building about twenty-five houses and two stores back home, and I had about a hundred men on. But I had some good foremen. I ended up building three churches in Newfoundland, one in St. John's, one in Corner Brook and one in Stephenville. Otis Keddy didn't want to stay, but he did, and in the end he built all three of them for us. He must have loved fishing.

Chapter 11
Three Churches and
a Trip

*Most of the projects I went into I had to
have faith—that was the only thing that
would keep us going. We had no money.*

BD

I got working with the people in Truro when they wanted to
remodel their church. It was pretty well a wreck and wasn't big
enough for them. They needed a new church but the committee
of about six or seven old-timers couldn't move. They wanted to
remodel, and they were sticking it out. The minister got to me
one night and asked what he should do. "Well," I said, "You need
a bigger committee. Bring in a lot of people with new thoughts;
you should have a committee of twenty-two, anyway." It was
quite a little while before he got them together, and at the first
meeting they voted for a new church. These young people had
been just chafing at the bit to get going and the old fellows were
holding them back.

The old church had a high steeple, and they wondered how to
get it down. So I told them we'd get a fellow to go up and put a

rope, about two-thirds of the way up on to it. There was a space of about thirty to forty feet between it and the next building and we had to land it there. We got hooked onto it, sawed the legs off down below, and tipped it over.

It smashed all to pieces, just into kindling wood, and the dust flew like smoke. They thought there was a fire. This black dust went up into the air and fell over everything. Some of the women down the street had clothes out on the lines, and they were some mad at us. I had never thought about the dust. About fifty or sixty people gathered around to watch it go down, and we all got black with the dust. They had a story in the paper about it.

At first we were going to build a wooden building. One night there was a meeting, and old Mr. Legge who ran Walker's Hardware in Truro was there. He was quite a supporter of the church. They had an old coal-burning furnace, and he would buy coal for them, things like that—the old-fashioned way of doing things. He was one of the people who didn't want to build a new church. He was so mad, he didn't want to speak to me for a while. He was even threatening to leave the church, and he was all hot and bothered about it. I had known him before, and he was a great old fellow, old Lee Legge. One time when I was building a church near Shubie, I sent a truck up to Truro to get some nails and all kinds of stuff from him. The staff felt they didn't know me well enough to give me credit, but they went to ask Lee who was in the basement. He shouted up, "Give him the whole store if he wants it. His credit is good with me."

Anyway, one day I went over to see him and he said, "Come up and have dinner with me." We talked for hours, and finally he said, "I guess I've got to give in, I'm old fashioned and I can't get over it, but if we didn't have you here, we wouldn't have a new church, so I'd better go along with you." He asked how much it would take to put brick on the church. I said twelve thousand dollars and he said, "Go ahead. I'll pay you for it." This was quite a lift. From then on, everything seemed to go ahead.

Ryan of Ryan Drug Store was another of the church members. He got so upset at one of the meetings where they decided to build a new church he had a heart attack. They had to take him home. He was right against it. Shortly after his wife died, I went over to see him. He said he wanted to give something in memory of his wife to the church. He said they were talking about caroline bells—would I get him a price on them. I said they were about six hundred dollars, and he said, "Well go ahead and order them and charge it up to me." From then on he was right up for the new church. It was things like that that clinched them together. I found that as a stranger I could go in and talk to them a lot better than some of their own people. They realized I was giving a lot of myself to these churches.

We had some of the same problems on P.E.I. But the people were very cagey. They didn't like anybody coming in, and I had quite a time. Pilan was a great little bricklayer who worked for me sometimes. He had done the Edgewood United in Halifax, and I took him over to the Island to build the First Baptist there. But they weren't going to let him do the brick work. "Well," I said, "If I'm going to stand behind it, I've got to have someone who I know is going to do good work." They chewed it over quite a bit and finally agreed. At that time they were building a government building just down the road out of brick. Three years later they had to tear out half of that brick work, and the Charlottetown Church was still as good as the day it was built. He was a great bricklayer. Harold Minton was pastor in Charlottetown and he gave me a lot of support during that time. Later he moved to Wolfville to become the head of the Divinity School at Acadia.

Harold Mitton

BD could move into a small struggling congregation, sense the pulse and talk to people and raise their consciousness about what they could do. That was one of the great services he rendered—it wasn't simply getting the building up. He moved amongst the people and inspired hope and faith and the courage to proceed. I was present at several meetings where the people had been absolutely sure they couldn't do anything. By the time BD got through telling them his homespun stories they'd be looking at one another and saying, maybe it's possible for us to do this. That was his great gift. I've seen a meeting change from defeatism to "Gosh, let's get going," and people hardly being able to wait to get out of there to get started.

BD didn't talk in highfalutin language. He talked the language of the people, and he used his humour and his stories. He didn't make a high profession of his faith. Mind you, he could be outspoken and tough on pastors, or anyone, if they appeared thick between the ears. But I never knew him to alienate anyone.

There was certainly nothing dour about him. Life wasn't easy for BD, but although he had many heartaches, with his sense of humour, his effervescence, his psychic energy, and his love of people, through it all, he triumphed.

I think that something that needs to be considered in any attempt to describe BD is that he regarded money as something to be used for the general good rather than to be piled up some place. He seemed set loose from material things and never seemed interested in accumulating wealth. At least, that was my experience.

And I don't think you could understand BD without understanding what Christian discipleship meant to him. I observed him a lot, and somewhere along the line, without being pretentious in any way, BD made a conscious commitment with his life, and he tried in his everyday life and in every area to put into practice what discipleship meant to him. Whenever he spoke there was a certain radiance about the man, and people always felt better for having been in his presence.

BD

One year we built a big Christian education building on the side of the West End Baptist in Halifax and remodelled the church completely. In those days you had to go early to get in—the crowd was so big. Even after we finished building it, it was full. They had something like eight hundred members. It was Abner

Langley who got me to go there and remodel it. They had no money to do anything, and everyone was frightened that if they got into debt, they could never repay it.

There were supposed to be some men there who would go good for a loan, but they all backed out. The bank manager was very leery as usual. He felt it was a pretty risky thing to do, because a church wasn't real security—you couldn't sell it. I had some property one place and another and I put it up for security. So after a bit of persuading, we borrowed the money. Abner and I went down to the bank and borrowed $75,000 to start the project in our own names. It was about a year before they started to pay me back. Most of the projects I went into I had to have faith—that's the only thing that would keep us going. We had no money.

Art Smith

BD reminded me quite a lot of R.A. Jodrey, as far as being smart goes. They had a lot of differences otherwise, but both of them were very keen men. BD was exceptional at adapting. He built my house here when several other builders couldn't see how it could be done. On the other hand, RA seemed to be able to smell a good deal. I remember one time he wanted to borrow seventy-five thousand dollars to buy shares in Crown Life. There was some opposition to it; he was always overdrawn, and their dividends were small. But RA said, "All I know is that they're doubling their sales every year." So they finally loaned him the money. In 1972 his investment was worth twelve million dollars and the Jodreys still control Crown Life. But you know, money never meant that much to BD. He got in tow with RA later with the nursing home. RA had bought a base from the Americans and figured he had made a mistake and was looking for a way to get out of it. But BD could see the possibilities.

Laurie Stevens

His debt-equity ratio was never intact; if it was debt or equity, it didn't matter. He borrowed it or he had it, and the two were the same. If he needed it for something he always figured he could pay it back somehow. People used to be shocked when he'd borrow for a church, but it didn't really bother him one way or the other. He would borrow from himself and pay it back, or he'd borrow from the bank. He wasn't really a dealmaker for himself.

BD

When we were remodelling the West End Baptist, Abner Langley was minister there, and we both worked awfully hard at it. I said, "When we're done, let's go on a vacation. Get someone to take over as minister and let's just go. I don't know where, but let's just get in the car and go away from here." We went to Boston first, and then decided to go on to New York. I told him before we started to pay all the bills, everything, and I'd give him the money to cover it. I said, "Whenever you're out, just let me know and I'll get you some more." He had never had money to spend like that in his life.

Abner loved to drive fast. I had a new DeSoto, and one time we were going so fast that when we stopped and left the car a while, the tires stuck to the road.

In New York we did pretty near everything you could think of. We went down to the piers about three in the morning and watched them unload the stuff they bring over from New Jersey to stock up New York for the day. We paid a man to show us around. We went to see a ball game, up the Empire State, and we went to Chinatown. We had to get someone to take us through there, too. You couldn't go alone, they were very suspicious.

I remember he wanted to buy a dress to take home for his wife and some books—he was crazy for books, always buying them. We stayed at the Statler Hotel, a nice place, and went everywhere by taxi. He said, "I never felt so much like a millionaire in my life." And it was the greatest trip of my life, too.

Laurie Stevens

He always worked hard, but once he went out and bought a new Cadillac. My mother was sick; she had had a stroke. He took her and my two young sisters all down through the States. That was a big thing for him—that was a statement. He bought this '54 Cadillac and away he went. I didn't find out until a month later. They just left.

After he and Abner had finished West End Baptist they took off. Both of them had worked night and day on that project and they thought they should go and do something else, like two bad kids. Every once in a while he'd do spontaneous stuff like that.

Abner Langley

It was a hilarious trip. We went into a big hotel, a nice hotel. You know BD could look and sound like a farmer on the back forty if he wanted to. The fellow in the hotel said he didn't have any low-cost rooms.

BD said, "I didn't say I wanted a low-cost room. What do you have in a good room." The fellow told him, and BD said, "Well, if that's all you've got, we'll take it." The fellow almost fainted.

He was always playing jokes. One Sunday on the way back we stopped for lunch at a restaurant and we were almost out of American money. BD said he had to do something and left first. I was supposed to pay but they wouldn't accept Canadian money. I got the manager and then the owner and spent nearly an hour and a half getting out of that restaurant. Right across the road was a large hotel with a big window in the lobby. BD was sitting there, waving at me whenever I looked at him, just smiling away. I was ready to shoot him. There was no sense to the trip, but it was one of the best trips I ever had, or he ever had. We still talk about it.

Chapter 12
Three More Churches

That's why I came here—to save
these people money.

BD

The Grace Memorial Church in Fredericton used to be on George Street. The church was falling apart but the old people didn't want to leave it. They wanted to get it fixed up, so they got me there different times to see what it would cost. Each time I tried to discourage them because they were right in the heart of the city with no houses around them, only businesses. They couldn't draw any new people. Everyone was building further out of town. After a while I persuaded them to at least think about a new church.

They wanted to know where to build it, so we went up on the side hill below the Trans-Canada Highway. There were big fields there, and one or two houses had been started. We thought it would be a good place. There was property there with some old shacks and an old house ready to be torn down, and it had a for-sale sign onto it. They wanted thirteen thousand for it, so I said, "I'll give you one thousand now and the rest when you get the deed ready." That same night there was a meeting, which was the reason I'd come, and they decided to hunt up a site to build on. I didn't say anything. They landed on this same piece of land and went to ask the price. The Trust Company who were handling it said they had sold it the day before to a man called Stevens. Well, they wanted to know what he was going to do with it and what his address was and began to inquire around. They tracked down an address on York Street, which was their minister's address, where I was staying. So that's how they got started on that piece of land.

They gave me permission to try to get some plans in Halifax. Mike Byrne had done some work for us—apartments and the like—and I asked him what it would cost. He said it would cost nine thousand to design and a lot to supervise the job. We agreed that I would supervise it for nothing which would save them ten thousand dollars. That's where we started.

Blair Williams

He got them to give him the deed to the old church and allowed them so much money for it. There was a manse and another old house they used for a Sunday School and an old barn, right on George Street, in downtown Fredericton. He knew exactly what he was going to do with it.

It was winter and he cleared a large space of snow and dumped two large loads of two-by-sixes next to the church. Some Jewish people were curious about what he was going to do there. This was just when Fredericton was starting to grow and developers were interested in buying. The church was short of money and he had a plan. He just put out the bait; that's how he operated, believe me. These fellows came and asked him what he was going to do. "Well," he said, "I'm going to take the church, and I'm going to cut the steeple off. Then I'm going to go high enough to make three floors, and I'm going to make twelve apartments out of it. And I'm going to make three apartments in the old manse. The old barn and the Sunday school, I'm going to tear down. Where you see all those shrubs and a nice lawn and privet hedge, I'm going to make a park."

"And what are you going to do then?"

"I'm going to rent them out when I get it finished."

That afternoon they had another visit; they said they were interested in buying. "Well," he said, "I don't know," and he gave them some figures on what it would cost per unit. "But," he said, "If you want it, I want sixty-five thousand dollars right now, as down payment." The next morning he had it, and he fixed the papers. He told me, "We can get on with the church now and wait till spring to start those apartments." It was just like setting a trap for a fox, putting that lumber there.

Freeman Fennerty

He sees an opportunity and seizes it right at the moment. One time he was flying to Fredericton to meet with the finance committee, and there was still a lot of money to raise. He sat next to a man who was an executive of an insurance company, and he got talking about financing buildings. BD asked if they ever lent money to churches. Well, the man didn't know but offered to check, and phoned the next day to say they would. So BD arranged for him to come and present it to the church. It was such a casual thing but it was typical of him—to talk with a man and put two and two together and find a way to move things forward.

BD

We were planning to put brick on the outside when one day the agent for angelstone came by. He said he'd like to see angelstone on it. Of course, I knew him well. I said we couldn't afford it but it would be a good advertisement for the company if they gave it to us. He said, he'd do some talking onto it. And it wasn't a week later, he came to say if we paid the freight, they would send it.

I found a couple of Swedish fellows who were real stonemasons, and they did a lovely job. You could just see that church grow when they started to put stone onto it. Today it would costs a fortune to have it done.

Blair Williams

When he first went to Fredericton, he wasn't known and didn't have credit. It used to annoy him when they wouldn't take his cheques and made things difficult. But he got established before long. One day I passed out all the cheques for the week—there must have been twenty-five or so—but they were not signed. On payday, Mr. Stevens used to come for lunch with us and sign the cheques but this day we forgot. I picked them up and never looked at them, and passed them all out. They were cashed, every one of them, and all over too: at Canadian Tire and the grocery store everywhere—even a few at the bank.

BD was in his bank in Halifax when some of them came through, and they thought it was quite a yarn. They said he must be well known, didn't even have to sign his cheques. BD said, "When I first went to Fredericton, they wouldn't take my cheques and now I don't even need to sign them."

Wanda Williams

You can see how we might have forgotten. We didn't have an office; we used our livingroom. I don't think he was ever the kind to sit down behind a desk. If he had cheques, to sign he'd sign them standing up. We had three small children at the time aged three, five and seven. It was busy. The youngest used to call him "BD Mr. Stevens." I never found him hard to work for. I did all the books, payroll and correspondence for the three churches in New Brunswick. He was a friend—that's all I can say about him.

Blair Williams

When we came to tear down the old steeple it was all planned. We had it all rigged up with a rope so that it would swing down between the wires and land on the sidewalk. I said it would be some tricky if it tipped over too far and took the wires with it. "Well," he said, "if it does, we will just have to pay for them." He had lots of nerve.

We had arranged to do it early Saturday morning, and we had police block off the roads. We had a chain-saw and a great big rope, and we got it hooked on the top of the steeple. We tied it back so he could cut it with an axe at the right time. A lot of people knew what we were going to do, and they were lined up watching.

The steeple fell down right on the sidewalk and never touched a wire. I thought his plan worked pretty good, so did everyone else. But what a mess: dirt, and pigeons, and sparrows flew out, and we even found a 1902 Eatons catalogue. He was a great guy for planning ahead and he was pretty good at it.

I worked every night throughout the week, building churches, and I often worked Saturdays too. One Saturday, it had been awful hot and I'd worked all day pouring a big wall over at Grace Memorial Church. I was dirty and sweaty, and I came home and got all showered up for supper. I had just sat down when BD came in. He said, "Let's take a walk over to the church." It was about a block from where we were living. We walked over and around the building and looked it over, and I knew what was coming. "Let's get a bar and throw a couple of boards off and have a look at it." So I went and got a wrecking bar and a sledge hammer. We never stopped till we had it all stripped and it was about dark. I was just as dirty and sweaty, as if I'd worked all day and this was Saturday night. But I didn't say anything. He was sixty-five then and every now and again, you know, he'd take a spurt and want to do a little work like that.

BD loved horses. One summer evening we went to an exhibition where they had some horse races. Before each race they'd parade the horses and BD would try to pick the one he thought was best—and generally he picked it. When the two-year-olds came by the stands BD picked one and do you know, it set a track record that night. He really enjoyed those races, and enjoyed them without betting.

BD had never been to the races before, and the joke was that the deacons of the church were sitting right in front of us. He'd say, "Isn't that so-and-so down there?" There were quite a few of them, and they were doing an awful lot of running back and forth, buying their tickets on the races. BD was getting a great

97

kick out of that. We sat behind them all night and they didn't know. It was kind of funny.

BD wasn't a typical Baptist. His religion, as such, was not so much an organized religion. His religion was his life, or vice versa. BD's sport was building churches. He didn't gamble on horses; he gambled on building churches.

One day towards the end of our building, I was putting down the pews in the church and a guy came in and start flying off at me. Oh boy, he was wild. We'd gotten the pews from the Ottawa Valley and this guy didn't like it that BD had come from Nova Scotia and not bought in New Brunswick. I said, "Look, there's the man coming in right now, you go talk to him." BD just happened to be coming in at that moment.

BD said, "Come on over and I'll show you the prices. I got three quotes: one from Nova Scotia, one from New Brunswick, and one from Ottawa. The Ottawa price saved us quite a few thousand dollars. That's why I came here—to save these people money."

BD

While I was staying in Fredericton we built three churches: the Grace Memorial in Fredericton, the Hartland Church, and the Forest Hill Church in Saint John. Harry Rockwell was foreman at Hartland and Dick Milne was later foreman at Forest Hill.

I visited my daughter who lives in Fredericton a while ago and we went to church service. I had just stepped in the door when a woman came and threw her arms around me and kissed me and said, "My, we're so glad to see you. If it wasn't for you we wouldn't have a church." It is a big church; it holds six hundred people or more and has forty-two classrooms, three assembly halls and a big gym. I was there when they burned the mortgage. They had it appraised it at a million and a quarter; I built it for two hundred and eighty-three thousand dollars. They are building a bigger church now at Forest Hill. They started in I think with thirty-eight members, and last I knew they had five or six hundred.

It's the funniest thing how you find people sometimes. I had bought a piece of land in Dartmouth which was mostly woods. I cut it off and took the lumber to a mill and had it sawed. The fellow who did the sawing was Dick Milne; his aunt owned the mill. He said they were going to shut down and would I have a job for him after he was finished sawing the lumber. He said, "I'm not much of a carpenter, but I'd like to learn."

At the time I was building a hall for men on the Oxford Street Church, and the foreman there was Harry Rockwell. I said, "Harry, here's a fellow who wants to learn the carpentry trade and wants to work." Harry said, "I don't know about learning him carpentry, but I can certainly give him lots of work." So Dick started there. He was only there a few days when they called me in about the church at Forest Hill in Saint John.

By the time we were ready to go in Forest Hill, Dick had been with us a couple of months, and I asked him to go to Saint John and build a church there. "Oh gracious," he said, "I couldn't do nothing like that."

"Yes, you could. I'll get you a trailer, and you and your wife can go right over and live. All you have to do is boss the job."

He was the best fellow you could ever have got to go there. He had never worked much at carpentry work, but he was very handy. He went over and did a real good job for me. The people thought the world of him. When it came time to finish up and build the pulpits, he built one there, another for Grace Memorial, and a third for Hartland. He is now our maintenance man at the nursing home.

Harry Rockwell, the foreman at Oxford Street, and then Hartland, weighed about 250 pounds. He was a big fellow and very easy-going. He said, "We didn't have carpenters at Hartland so we built the church with potato pickers." By the time he got through with them he had them pretty near like they were carpenters. He was a great worker. I'd no sooner get to Hartland than something would go wrong at Fredericton and I'd have to go right back. But I had good men on the job.

Chapter 13
Beaverbank
Nursing Home

I was getting weary at that time....
But I still thought I could do some-
thing for people when we started in
on the nursing home.

Blair Williams

The Beaverbank Nursing Home project started in Fredericton. He knew R.A. Jodrey had bought the base from the Americans and we got talking about it. He said, "Jeepers that would be a great thing for something like a nursing home." He was going to build one down in Windsor at the time. There were a lot of handicapped and retarded people who would soon not have a place to go when the place in Halifax closed, and that gave him an idea.

Next time we talked he said, "With RA's money and my ideas we could do a lot."

RA had bought the thing and likely got it cheap from the government and didn't know what to do with it. With some people the more money they make, the more they want but I think with Jodrey it wasn't really the money, I think it was the deal that was important. He was a deal maker. But they didn't know what to do with it and had to have someone like BD who was a builder, a creator. But I don't imagine RA lost anything on it. He wasn't known for losing too much. So the first time BD went back to Halifax he said they wanted us to buy it, and the next time he came back and said they had. He sold one of his apartment buildings to get the money to start.

BD

My first wife was a wonderful woman and then she had a stroke that affected her mind. She was very sick at the time. She had had a stroke and came out of it but it left her confused. You had to watch her. She'd clear out and go away. I should never have taken her to Fredericton by rights, because after I got there and got settled down, she got worse. I think she was confused to be away from home. She was always going home—but she couldn't find her home. I would just pray to the Lord to give me strength to look after her. I knew if it was me who was affected she would look after me.

Before we went to Fredericton, sometimes she used to get up in the night and want to go to Windsor where her old home was. One or two in the morning, she would get restless and want to go. I would take her there when we were in Halifax and she would go in and start doing the dishes or something, and after a little she would say, I guess they're all asleep, we might as well go home. And we would get in the car and go home and she would go right to sleep. She was that way for about eight years.

When I went to Fredericton to build Grace Memorial she always wanted to go home. She never wanted to be put in a home. She'd say, "I know I'm getting too sick to be here, but don't put me in a home."

Blair Williams

One night he had gotten up and he blacked out and fell and hit his head on the baseboard and was there towards morning when his wife found him, there on the floor. He was conscious but didn't exactly know where he was or what had happened to him. She was sick at the time and got flustered easily and often couldn't find her way. We were in the same building but at the other end, and she started off to find us but couldn't and got all mixed up. Someone took her back and they managed to phone us. I went up and found Mr. Stevens sitting on the bed and the side of his face was just all black. We got him to the hospital and found out he had diabetes. He wasn't too well, and there were times he drove himself too hard.

BD

There were times there when we were busy with the churches I couldn't see how the nursing home was going to go ahead. The banks wouldn't lend me the money, so I went to old Roy Jodrey and told him I couldn't finance it. He said, "I have money sitting in the bank only earning six percent. I'll lend it to you at that rate." Old Roy Jodrey was a great old fellow. He lent it to me. He had the property then and wanted to get rid of it. He asked if I felt I could make a go of it and when I couldn't find the money anywhere else, he lent it to me. I borrowed for the home and had to put some of my own money in to keep it afloat. I borrowed about six hundred thousand and put in about forty-two thousand dollars of my own money. It was all paid back in a few years. I had no security and borrowed against my reputation I guess.

We had two managers who lost us a lot of money in the early years. We had our ups and downs, lost forty-two thousand the first year. They had good ideas and wanted to help people, but they weren't business people. Wanted to make it just like their home. That's OK, but if you want to stay in business you have to set it up that way.

Buying materials was one thing they were lost on. The city wanted us to take 48 patients at short notice. Well, they wanted to buy new hospital beds at $150 to $200 apiece. I went down and put a bid on army-surplus hospital beds and got 100 for $3.00 a piece. They're still there. I got army-surplus blankets at

$6.00 and the last time I went out there they still had a few they hadn't used.

They wanted to send out the laundry but I went down to the V.G. hospital and bought their used stuff and set up our own laundry. They wanted five hundred dollars for them and they were worth seven thousand. We had a good maintenance man who kept them going.

It was Dick Milne who was our foreman over in New Brunswick when we built the church in Saint John. Saved them thousands. The laundry has been going ever since. That's the sort of thing you need to be successful and to keep things going. If you failed up, you wouldn't be there to help people for long.

Harry Renfree

I have one rather special memory of that time. I was general secretary of The Atlantic Baptist Convention. I'd had some business background and BD just casually mentioned to me one day that he was having a little difficulty with staff at the nursing home he had built out Sackville way. He asked me if I'd be interested in taking the position as manager. As usual he was very generous in the salary he suggested. I didn't think too long. I simply said to him that I didn't think that that was really my call at that point. He said, "I'd like you to take it but I didn't think you would. I admire you for it."

Laurie Stevens

My mother had had two or three strokes by the time they went to Fredericton. She had Alzheimer's and he moved her up there with him. They lived in a small apartment there but she was almost gone then, she was almost out of it at that time. But I don't think it hurt her that much. I'm sure he thought it did because she was often not well, and all of a sudden when they came back, she wasn't at all well. But I think it was just the natural progression of things. When she came back, she thought I was her brother.

Helen Thompson

And even after she took so sick and she couldn't talk, she always had communication with us. She'd either look at us, we knew what she wanted, or she'd take you by the hand, if you asked her questions and she'd answer by squeezing your hand. We always used to wonder if she was scared, and she'd say no. She was never scared. She gave everybody a lot of strength.

And she was always ready to help us, even though she was so sick. If something happened to one of us girls, it seemed like it snapped her right out her sickness. She could help you and then, maybe a day later, why she wouldn't even remember.

My mother had a very difficult time to adjust when she first came to Halifax. We had a large house in Windsor, and she looked after the home because Dad worked down here. He'd just come home on weekends. Then we moved to Halifax and she fixed up this so-called shanty, which was a garage really. Made it real comfortable. We didn't have too many walls. He had it studded off with three large bedrooms, but we used blankets for walls and we lived there from early spring until fall, when we moved in to the house he was building. He had built some on it before we came, but he decided if we were to come, then he wouldn't lose the weekends. She liked to see everything nice and she worked hard fixing that place up, then when we moved in the main house, she still had to work hard.

She always went to church. My father wasn't a good church-goer until later in life. Even as young children, when we could just walk and it took us a half an hour from our home in Windsor to the Baptist Church, she always had to go. And when we moved down to Halifax, she was only here a short time when she had to find a church for us to attend. So we went to St. John's Anglican and that's where we got most of our bringing up.

My father was a man who never ever kept books. All his books was in his head. She didn't approve of that. She always told us, "No matter what you do, or if you have money, you can always balance your books in a scribbler or note pad." She would get my father to sit down with her and he'd say he spent this and he spent that, and she'd say, "Burnett, that's too much. We have to leave a little for the children." She always kept it in a scribbler.

He was building houses and he was buying stuff and she used to keep all his records in a big book. Each house, she'd have everything listed, everything that went into that house. Now it's just an old book, but she had her credits and her debits and her balance and that's what she worked off. She didn't have any bookkeeping, but she had her education.

If she was troubled about something, she had to go and find the reason why. She needed to know herself. Even after I was married, she'd come and say, "You have to drive me such-and-such a place," and we'd say, "What is she going to do now?" Then we'd say, "Do you want us to go in with you?"

"No, I just want you to wait here in the car. I'll just be a few minutes."

And she'd go in and do her business, and when she came out, she'd be just as happy as when she went in. You'd never know, she'd never say anything but she just had to know, herself.

To us, my mother was always very happy. She never complained. She never hollered at us. But when she spoke, we knew what she meant. My father would come home and he'd bring somebody. He never let her know until he walked through the door and then he'd say, "Eva, we're having company for supper." Well, you know, with five children then and only so much to go on, she would call us aside and say, "Girls, you have to share tonight." Well, that didn't mean too much, you know. We could take most anything but she'd set the table and we'd all sit down, very pleased, and she'd be very happy and talk with them. And of course, us kids were all looking at each other to see how much she had taken out of each plate. If we were looking too much, well, she would look at us and sort of smile, and we knew.

When he was away at the mills, we'd say could we go somewhere, and she'd say, "How are you going to learn that you don't like it if you don't try." She never told us to go, and she never told us to stay home, but that is the way she'd always put it. We didn't realize how much influence she had over us or him, until we got older.

He'd come home and he'd walk in from the camps and he was always so busy, he'd say, "Clear the kids out. I have to talk to you." She didn't think that was right, but she never ever told him. She'd say, "Girls, you can go into the dining room." Well, the dining room was next to the kitchen so we heard everything anyway. It was always that way. But that's the way my father always did things, and she always accepted it, although some- times if it got a little much she would call him aside. We never heard them fight or argue, but she'd say, "Burnett, we have to have a talk." And when she called him Burnett, we knew we had to scamper somewhere.

When my father got in with people during the war, and he was real busy because he had all the war houses, the pre-fabs, to put up, she kept her little brood all together. It wasn't a little brood by that time, because three more happened along. Then he decided that he was going to move into the Maples, which was a larger house, and that is where she started to put her foot down a bit. My father brought everybody to the big house. The door was always open for anybody, but she had to have time for herself, but she confided in us more, the three older girls, after we moved into the Maples. And it used to make us mad that she wouldn't argue or stick up for herself, but she said no, that was her life and that's they way she wanted it. If she was mad, she'd always sing a little bit. We always knew if something was wrong. She'd be washing the dishes and humming along, al- ways humming.

When you went in the room with her, if you had trouble, she was very peaceful and calm and, all of sudden, you didn't have troubles. When we went to her, she'd sit there and she'd listen to you, and then she'd say, "You know, you mustn't have been reading your Bible lately, have you?" You'd just feel like two cents because maybe you hadn't, but I mean then she'd talk and she'd tell you and when you'd come out, why you'd feel like nothing was wrong at all.

Herb Saulnier who worked with Dad for over forty years, knew her, but most of the others didn't. He said if Dad hadn't had her behind him, he wouldn't be where he is today. All the men were very kind to her and the office was right in her home, so she didn't have that much privacy for her own company. She never ever pushed him, she just kept him on track. He knew when she spoke to him that he was maybe wrong because often he never thought. My father never thought of anything until it was too late. He'd do something on the spur of the moment and come home and tell her and she'd say, "Oh, my."

"Oh well, it's done now."

He wasn't thinking of anybody but only in just getting the job done. Well, that wasn't her way. She had to think of the person that it was going to hurt. He was like that right through his life, and she accepted it. She used to say, "Well, I married your father, didn't I?" When my brother was born, she took very sick, and after he passed away, she never really got better after that.

My father decided that he would build a house for her after she took real sick. She always came to our house after I was married, and she even lived with us a lot because he was never home. So he decided he would build her a house just behind us. She even watched him build it, but he never told her it was for her. One night she was sitting here in the room—she loved her grandchildren, so she used to sit here and talk—and one night she said, "I think I'm going to have to have words with your father."

"Well, you go right ahead. We'll go out."

"No, you don't need to go out, but I think he's doing something behind my back."

Well, that sort of gave us a shock. Anyway, it was her birthday and Dad came and said, "Eva, I have a surprise for you. I built you a house right in back of Helen and Butch."

"Well, I don't want to live there," she said. "I don't want to interfere with their lives and that is too handy. I want to live right where I am, in the Maples."

So he had to turn around and build a little house on the bottom lot, where she used to have raspberry bushes. And she was quite happy there, but she used to take little strokes and the like and from there on in, they had to have maids looking after her. But even through her sickness, she never complained, she never changed.

I think she had that spiritual quality more than my father. She was the one that carried it. I don't think Dad really knew her. I don't, to be real honest, think he knew. He'd always say, "Your mother is a good woman. Listen to her." But I don't think he knew what she was really like. It wasn't until she was real sick that he had to live with her and even then she was quiet and she enjoyed herself.

BD

I was getting weary even at that time, getting too old to go around building churches or anything else much. I was getting to the place where I couldn't do much more ... I'd have to stay home with Eva most of the time. But I still thought I could do something for people when we started in on the nursing home. When the time came when I couldn't look after my wife at home, I built a piece on to the nursing home and we went to live out there. She spent the last year and a half of her life out there. The nurses were some good to her. That was twenty years ago or more.

Chapter 14
Tapering Off

There were times when I didn't see how I could do some of these things, but I kept on.

Freeman Fennerty

After I left Newfoundland and came back to Kentville, the next time I worked with BD was at Mt. Uniacke where I had been asked to do some church work. He became interested partly because it was a new thing and partly because I was there. He transferred his membership there and undertook to build the new church. He used to do that—move his membership, which meant his tithing, wherever he was interested in getting started. He wanted to be right where the action was. He really supervised the project. From the beginning, he was involved in the whole thing. He was at least eighty.

BD

If I was going to build a new church, I generally took my membership and my tithing with me, because then you could sit in on the board and you could speak; otherwise, you just had to wait until someone else told you what had happened. It was to the benefit of the church as well as for me to bring my tithe.

Freeman Fennerty

Later we did something that probably we wouldn't have done under other circumstances. We made a survey ourselves around Elmsdale. We went round and told people we were interested in starting a new church there. And then we found a site and we bought it. Well, you know, we were both old and life runs out.

Reg Short

I was chairman of the Home Missions Board and BD wanted to get me familiar with what was going on in Elmsdale. So he called up and asked me to go for a drive to look at some land with Freeman. It was snowing hard, but that didn't matter; we went anyway. He drove all around, pointing out all the houses and the churches and how many people they would hold. He said the churches couldn't even handle one-tenth of the people on a Sunday morning. Then we came to a piece of land and he asked me what I thought. Well, I thought it was a good site—just between the main areas of population—and I could see a church there. "Well, we bought it." he said, "And the deed's in the hands of the Home Missions Board, or will be shortly. Now we have to get some money to build the church." He was really feeding me with all this information to get it to the board.

It snowed and it snowed and it snowed and we were driving around in his brand new Buick. By the time we got to the MicMac Rotary everything was plugged solid. I said, "You fellows better get back home and I'll walk from here." I'll never forget it as long as I live. BD never thought of BD. I think that was the last person he ever thought of. He was in his eighties then.

BD

That Reg Short is a comical fellow. One day after his mother had died he dropped in to see me. He said he had his mother in the car and he was taking her around to see the sights one more time and he just snorted with laughter. She had been cremated and he did have her in the back of his car.

In Elmsdale about eight people were interested in another church, and we formed a church with those eight as officers. There were forty-two members in just a year. But before we got the church organized, Freeman and I bought the lot of land for seventeen thousand dollars. He put in two thousand and I put in fifteen thousand dollars. We told people about it after we had bought the land. We put a big sign on the property: "This is the site of the new Baptist church." I got it paid back now, but we owed thirty-eight thousand on the church, and now we have to borrow forty-five thousand for the parsonage. It's quite a load for the people. They're real good givers; they're used to tithing and most give ten percent of whatever they're earning to the church.

Freeman Fennerty

A man with BD's ability and size of business could have become very selfish. There are people whose goal is to accumulate wealth and manipulate people, but being a Christian—and a very practical Christian at that—BD didn't do that. Things had to be done to a certain standard or they wouldn't be done. He had a way of getting the best out of people and giving them responsibility. And often with a sense of humour, too.

I remember he was talking to a businessman who was moaning and telling him that things weren't going too well. BD said, "You have been trying to run your own life for quite a long time and you haven't done such a good job. Why don't you give the Lord a chance?" On the other hand he could take the other side. I once heard him tell a man who was being overly dogmatic about something: "You're so heavenly, you're no earthly use."

Wayne Langley

The things that sticks in my mind is that he seemed to have no social life at all but that he was a very social person. Only once in the thirty years I knew him did I see him in a social setting. He and my dad had many many meetings, but there was no spare time. Just before his second wife died, his eyesight had him very limited. He was just at the end of being able to drive and very frustrated with it, but his desk was still full of correspondence which he laboured to read.

There was not a whimper and he never seemed down, although he had lots of reason to be. He never seemed to have any excuses for himself like, "I don't have time," or "It can't be done." I never heard those things. He carried that openness with him and he was, I don't know, like a rock.

BD

I helped to build a little church at Stevens Road, a subdivision we developed in Dartmouth. I gave them the land and built the first church while we built all the houses on the subdivision. It was just a little house, which we later used as a parsonage, but it wasn't big enough for a church. When Laurie built his house there he built a new church for them. They called it Stevens Road Church after me.

Reg Short

When we were building Stevens Road Church, Laurie got the men involved with finishing the inside, which brought them together as a fellowship. We had put the outside frame up and it was roof-tight and we decided to move from the little wooden building into the basement at Christmas time. The first Sunday we all sat there with our overcoats on, it was that cold. The congregation was almost doubled on Christmas Day, so we said the secret was to get out of the little building and finish building the church. "Well," Laurie said, "we could do it if we could get ten thousand dollars. I need ten guys who will sign a note for one thousand at the bank. So ten of us went down and signed the note."

Betty Short

Reg wouldn't have been able to do that if he hadn't been taught. So you could see BD's influence even then.

Reg Short

I'm telling you it was a scary thing, because you knew the bank could call any time. If the church didn't grow and pay it off, what would we do? You could lose your home. A thousand dollars in those days was equal to ten thousand today. We had no spare money around. Anyway, we borrowed it, finished the inside of the church, moved in, and paid the loan off in one year.

BD

Sometimes a minister doesn't prove to be very good. One fellow we had was a retired serviceman. He was a little too military, and the church didn't grow like it should have. He got a pension and another bit of money from the church as well as a free house and car—about equal to twenty-five thousand dollars a year. He was a good preacher but he didn't have the heart; he hardly ever called amongst the people. He stayed six years and pretty near ruined the church. You know, people will impose on you if you don't stand up to them. Church people are no exception.

Rev. Donald Thomas

The day our church in New Glasgow burned, we were away on a picnic. I was cooking some hamburgers, and I saw a Mountie driving towards me and I thought, "Now what's that Mountie doing? Why is he coming here? Is he going to tell me to put this fire out?" But he came over and said, "Are you Reverend Thomas?"

"Yes."

"Well, your church is on fire."

"You mean the house, don't you."

"No, the church."

When he said that I just dropped everything and took off. You could see the flames, and the whole thing caved in and bang-o, we were... I felt, I don't know, everything went out of my life.

The next morning Dr. Oliver called me. He said, "I was talking to BD Stevens and he's interested in talking to you." So I told him we were having a meeting the following night. He called BD and told him and BD said he would be there. Sure enough he was.

At that very first meeting BD said, "You lost the building but you still have the church." And that was true if you think about it. That gave us the incentive to go ahead and do all we could to see that we had a new church structure. He came and gave us new faith to go ahead and build a new church for our people.

He told us, "I'm here and I'll help you build a new church if you're interested." We were interested in buying a new piece of property. The man who owned it offered to sell us a small piece for fifty thousand dollars, but we found out that that was what he had paid for the whole seven and one half acres. We said, "No, we are not going to be taken that way." We saw other pieces and hemmed and hawed and finally decided that maybe we could build on the same land if we could get planning permission and the approval of the fire marshall. Then we called BD again. He came down and measured it out and said, "Okay, we can build this size and this shape church on this piece of land." And then he took it to the planning commission and the fire marshall.

Freeman Fennerty

BD's eyesight wasn't so good in those days. He couldn't sit down and read much. He could only watch TV a certain amount. All he could do was sit and think, and that was bad for a man of his past activity. I could see the frustration setting in. When the Baptist church in New Glasgow burned and they came to him to ask for advice, I never dreamed he could do what he did. He drew plans for them and then undertook to put up the building. Then I saw a whole new lease on life as he began to work on the church.

Rev. Donald Thomas

BD did all the leg work, every bit of it, once we gave him the okay. He said, "I'll do it, and I'll charge you one dollar for my services." And sure enough, he brought down a trailer and stayed in it and went home weekends. He drew up the plans and then turned around and bought all the lumber. He gave out all the contracts for the foundation and told them, each one of them, what to do, how to make it, and so on. Each day at ten in the morning you could be sure he would arrive on the scene. And he would be on the phone to me most every day. He would see the men, and afterwards my wife would always have a pot of tea and crackers and cheese for him. Every Wednesday she'd give him his lunch.

As the work went on, one evening BD took every one of the workers plus their wives out to supper. He had the dining-hall of the Heather Motel reserved for all of us and paid it all himself. He was the greatest man I ever met to practice his Christianity.

The day of the dedication came and BD gave the keys to the chairman of trustees. Then we paid him a dollar. We gave him a silver dollar. He was eighty-five at the time.

BD

I put a lot of my own money into these churches over the years. I figured that if I had the money, it was about the best investment I could make, and I think it was. There were times when I didn't see how I could do some of these things, but I kept on. You have to make sure you are on the right track first, and then you have to stick to it no matter what.

You have to have a strong urge never to give up. I was never disappointed in people. I took it for granted that people had their lives to live, same as me, and that I shouldn't expect them to live just the way I wanted. But you can help people to change. I was seldom discouraged in my life; my faith has held me over.

Laurie Stevens

Dad went to Fredericton to see my sister. It was a long drive and he wanted to go, but he ended up in hospital. They thought he had a constriction in his bowel and operated. They found it wasn't, just a kind of twist which was blocking things, maybe from the five-hour drive. Anyway I went up to see him and it just turned out that we were all there, all six daughters and me. He was lying on his back with all those tubes and intravenous bags hanging above him and when we came in he said, "Who's there? Hand me my glasses so I can see."

"We're all here."

"You are?"

"Yes, all of us."

"I can't see lying here. Nurse, I'm just going to get that young fellow to lift me over to that chair so I can see these people."

"I don't think you should to do that, Mr Stevens."

"You're much too young to be telling me what to do, miss."

Well, we got him over to the chair with all his tubes and everything and he just sat there smiling.

"This is so nice, I think I'll have my lunch here."

"I don't think the doctor would want you to do that, Mr. Stevens."

"Well, this won't be the first time I've done things I shouldn't do. It's wonderful to see you all here. If I'd expected this I'd have got sick sooner."

He died two days later of complications from the operation. He never should have made that trip, but he wanted to go. The spirit was there to the very end.

Afterword

Harry Renfree

BD Stevens was, without a doubt, one of the finest men I ever met. I counted him as a very close friend and indeed as a man who had a major influence on my own life. If nothing else he taught me the true meaning of Christian stewardship, for his own generosity and dedication down through many years were remarkable.

BD was a kind of homespun philosopher who told me on more than one occasion that his money belonged to God and that was the way he lived his life.

He was one of the greatest church builders in the Atlantic provinces—and not only the physical buildings but also of the church that is made up of people. As far as the Baptists are concerned, he was the greatest church plant builder we have ever had historically in all of Canada. He built over 30 churches. And he did not only build for the Baptists.

BD was a man of vision, but his greatest contributions were personal.

Epilogue

It is not often one gets to interview one's great grandfather. This is the transcript of an interview done for a school project on Heritage Day by BD's great grandson, Andrew Giffen, who was in grade one, February 20, 1988.

Andrew: I am having an interview with my great grandfather, BD Stevens, who was born in the year 1900. Grandad, did you have any chores to do after school?

BD: Oh yes. We had lots of chores. We used to have to get the wood and chop it up and get it ready for the next day. And we had to go and feed the cows and hens and collect the eggs.

Andrew: Grandad, how big was your school?

BD: We had about 30 in our school. We had a teacher who was an awful nice old teacher. She used to bring lunches for us sometimes because we was very poor those days. We didn't have much to eat.

Andrew: Grandad, did you have a school bag to carry your books in?

BD: We carried them under our arm and used to get in a fight and lose our books.

Andrew: Grandad, What did you have for recess?

BD: Oh we had an apple or something like that. We hardly ever had very much for recess.

Andrew: Grandad, what games did you play?

BD: Well, we played hopscotch, skipping, and all kind of little games.

Andrew: Grandad, what was it like in winter in school?

BD: Very cold in our school house. We just had a great big potbellied stove set in the middle of the room and we had to carry the wood in to put into it to keep us warm. The snow lots of years was very deep.

Andrew: Grandad, did you have lots of friends at school?

BD: Oh yeah. We were all friends at school. Sometimes we'd get in fights and one thing and another but most of the time we were good friends.

Andrew: Grandad, did you live in a big house?

BD: Yes. It was an old farm house. It was very cold in the winter and we had a hard time to keep it warm. There was eight of us children all at home and we used to have to get the wood in to keep the house warm.

Andrew: Grandad, how did you get to the school in the mornings?

BD: We walked there. We were very close to the school. The school was just over across the street from us.

Andrew: Grandad, how big was your school?

BD: Our school was very small. It was called the little red school house. There was just room for us all to get in.

Andrew: Grandad, what did you have to write with?

BD: We had a slate and a pencil and we wrote on the chalk board with chalk. We didn't have no paper or scribblers in those days.

Andrew: Grandad, what classes did you have?

BD: I think we had eight different classes. Started in grade primary and went clear up to grade twelve. The one teacher taught them all.

Andrew: Grandad, what was the most popular game back then?

BD: We used to play marbles an awful lot and they'd fight over who got the big marble. That's the way we played.

Andrew: Grandad, what did you wear back then?

BD: My mother made all our clothes and made leggings for our feet instead of shoes. They were made out of leather. That's all the shoes we had in those days. Most of the time in the summer we went in our bare feet because we couldn't afford shoes.

Andrew: Thank you Grandad for the interview.

BD: Oh, you're welcome.